EXTERNAL BALLISTICS FOR RIFLE SHOOTING

EVERYTHING YOU NEED TO KNOW ABOUT EXTERNAL

BALLISTICS TO HIT AT ANY DISTANCE

JONATAN SJÖSTEEN

1st Edition (2024)

ISBN 978-91-531-1224-2

INTRODUCTION

External ballistics is a well-developed science. We know a lot about the factors that affect a projectile's flight through the air, and we have learned to compensate for them very well. Modern computer technology has allowed us to accurately model ballistic trajectories, even at very long distances. However, there is not much literature that expresses external ballistic phenomena and effects in ways that are easy to understand without being an aeronautical engineer or ballistician. When we read more advanced ballistics literature, we often find that it is filled with mathematical formulae. That is great if we're programming a ballistic calculator, but not so great if we're a hunter or competitive shooter who wants to know how external ballistics works in practice. In this book I illustrate with many examples how different kinds of external ballistic phenomena affect different rifle calibers in practice. In this way, a shooter can quickly get an idea of whether a particular external ballistic phenomenon is important for his or her type of shooting or not.

I once heard the distinguished American journalist and author Thomas E. Ricks say that the only good reason to write a book is that you have to. I don't know if that is true in general, but it is certainly true for me as I write this book. I took up competitive rifle shooting a number of years ago, and I didn't realize when I started it just how difficult it is. At the same time that I was appalled by all the things we have to know and understand, I was also fascinated by the fact that we can learn to compensate for atmospheric phenomena and hit what we want at very long ranges. Once we have learned to compensate for the main effect on the projectiles path, which is gravity, it is usually the wind that causes problems when shooting. Wind is something I hope to give you tools to understand and deal with in this book. Here are a few questions that swirled in my head and compelled me to write this book: how much does air pressure affect the trajectory? How does temperature affect air pressure? Why does gyroscopic drift occur, and how significant is it? What is the Coriolis effect? I have an inquisitive mind, and after a few months without satisfactory answers to these and many other questions, I realized that I had to sit down and write down everything I knew, or thought I knew, and everything I didn't know, do the research, and then come up with something. The result is in front of you.

This book is not extensively footnoted throughout the text. Instead, in the end of the book you will find the scientific literature that underpins my basic understanding of exterior ballistics. The most fundamental modern work of exterior ballistics is perhaps *Modern Exterior Ballistics: The Launch and Flight Dynamics of Symmetric Projectiles* by Robert L. McCoy. McCoy has been called the father of modern ballistics, and his book is undoubtedly an indispensable work in this field. McCoy's book is not, however, very accessible to a hunter or sport shooter trying to understand exterior ballistics. Another distinguished author in the field is Bryan Litz, author of *Applied Ballistics for Long Range Shooting*, documenting Litz's experience and lessons learned during years of research into primarily long-range shooting. Litz's work has been invaluable in transferring his expert ballistic knowledge to the general shooting population. However, after reading much of the work by established authors in the field, I was still lacking information about, for example, the theory of engaging moving targets, and found that it was mostly geared to a Northern American readership, exemplified with Imperial units of measure. I still felt that a comprehensive work was lacking, that both exemplifies in ways that are easy to understand, more deeply explains the physical phenomena that dictate exterior ballistics, and gives the reader practical advice to apply the theory in practical shooting situations. This is the kind of work that I looked for when I first started out in competition shooting, and that I have attempted to produce. A work that is accessible to the layman shooter, as well as comprehensive and thorough enough to also be interesting for someone who is already knowledgeable in the field.

The subtitle of this book is "Everything you need to know about external ballistics to hit at any distance". There are a couple of potentially controversial word choices in this subtitle: "everything" and "any distance". I wrote "everything" because my intention is actually to include everything a rifle shooter needs to know about external ballistics in order to hit at the distances you want to. That is the goal of this book. Regarding distances, my goal with this book is to provide you with the knowledge you need to shoot at any distance whether it's 200, 500 or 2500 meters or yards. The complexity increases with increased shooting distance, as external ballistic effects have a greater impact later in the trajectory, and some additional factors that have negligible impact at shorter distances come into play. My ambition is to give you the knowledge you need to succeed in shooting, no matter what your rifle discipline is.

When I started writing this book, I had intended to write only about external ballistic effects on projectiles in long-range shooting. However, while writing it, I felt it necessary to occasionally make some remarks about internal ballistics and ammunition. The reason is simple: ammunition is one of the most important variables in rifle shooting. There is a reason why military snipers have ammunition that is specifically manufactured and adapted to their weapon systems: they want total control over how the ammunition functions in their rifles. The same applies to competitive shooters (with the exception of those cartridges that cannot be hand-loaded). Most serious precision shooters load their own ammunition. The more consistent the quality of the ammunition, the better the results will be at all distances, and especially long ones.

Table of Contents

WHO IS THIS BOOK FOR?

This book is aimed at both beginners in rifle shooting, as well as more experienced shooters who want to take their understanding of external ballistics to the next level. My ambition with the book has been to start by providing a basic understanding of external ballistics for rifle shooting, and the influencing factors that are relevant at different distances, and then to weave in more advanced ballistics for those who want to understand the mathematical formulae and constituent variables.

Even for the shooter who already has a thorough understanding of external ballistics and who has read extensively on the subject, I believe there is useful information in this book, such as details about Coriolis or Eötvös drift, tools and strategies for managing wind drift, or presenting formulas in metric measurements instead of the usual Imperial units of measure. This type of literature tends to be dominated by American works, as the Americans are leading the way in shooting, so the formulae in books on shooting and ballistics are almost always written in Imperial units of measure. I have converted many of the formulas in the book to metric units from the American units of measurement. This doesn't mean, of course, that the book isn't directed towards American readers. A lot of shooters in the US already use metric values, and the angular measurement milliradian, when they practice precision shooting.

This book is also more thorough in its physical explanations of external ballistic phenomena than many other books on external ballistics. A book on ballistics aimed at a broader readership than physicists must also be presented in a way that does not require extensive prior knowledge of mathematics or physics. It should not be too scientific but neither too general nor mundane. This is a difficult balance. Personally, I find that many books on shooting are too layman-like and not detailed enough in their physical explanations of the phenomena. This is of course a personal preference, as some shooters are only interested in *what happens*, rather than *why it happens*. I am interested in both.

DISPOSITION

The chapters in the book are organized so that the first part gives a general description of how an external ballistic phenomenon affects the bullet trajectory at different distances, with examples for common rifle calibers. Later in the chapters is discussed in more detail why different phenomena occur, what their physical mechanisms are, and also how to calculate to compensate for them. By dividing the chapters in this way, the reader can gain a direct understanding of an external ballistic phenomenon without having to read formulas and get out their calculator. Those who are interested in the physical explanations and the mathematics behind them, on the other hand, can read on to satisfy their appetite.

I have designed the disposition of this book so that it is not necessary to study the included ballistic tables to get a grasp of the importance of a certain external ballistic factor. I think too many ballistic tables can disturb the reading experience. The book does, however, contain ballistic tables that exemplify the effect of external ballistic factors. The ballistic tables are not the heart of the book, but rather the basis for discussing various external ballistic factors and their effects and importance for shooting. I intended to publish this book both as an e-book and as a print book. The truth is that ballistic tables, that I use to exemplify many of the external ballistic phenomena, are not that suitable for the e-book format. Some of them are rendered small and difficult to read. Because of the specific file format of e-books, there is not much I could do about this. The tables and graphics look much better in the print version.

This book was originally written in Swedish, and then translated into English. The Swedish version of this book uses metric units of measurement. In the English version of the book, the metric ballistic tables are either modified to include imperial measurements, or imperial ballistic tables are added so there are both metric and imperial tables. The ballistic examples should thus be easily comprehensible for both a European and a North American readership. The discussions about external ballistic effects generally include both metric and imperial measurements for the same reason. A lot of precision shooters, even in North America, are already used to thinking in terms of metric measurements and milliradians because it is the most widespread system used worldwide for this purpose. In discussions regarding wind speed or distance, I have also added miles per hour and yards in order to simplify an intuitive understanding for a North American readership.

Conversion tables for all kinds of measurements that are used in a shooting context can also be found in the end of the book. The ballistic examples in this book should be relatable for most readers, since they are based on common calibers such as 6.5 Creedmoor, 6.5x55 Swede, .308 Winchester, .300 Winchester Magnum, .338 Lapua Magnum and others.

In the book I often refer to different shooting ranges, such as "short distances", "medium distances", "long distances" and "very long distances". These terms are admittedly a bit dubious to use, because their general understanding is quite arbitrary. What is a long distance for a deer hunter will hardly even be sighting-in distance for a competitive long-range shooter. It is therefore a bit precarious to use such terms in this context without defining them more in detail. Granted, such a definition will probably differ from person to person, and is in no way meant to be the definitive truth. I will allow myself a rudimentary definition of these terms, as they are used in this book and need to be defined. This working definition is influenced by what I consider to be a general approximate understanding of shooting distances, as well as the state of rifle shooting and the relevant distances today. I am well aware of the potential pitfalls of trying to define shooting distances, since the longest competitive shooting ranges today are more akin to military mortars than hunting distances, and the technology is constantly moving forward. For the purposes of this book, I consider a very short shooting distance to be <100 meters/109 yds), short distances 101-300 meters (appr. 110-300 yds), medium distances 301-600 meters (appr. 301-650 yds), long distances 601-1000 meters (651-1100 yds) and everything above those very long distances. And I do apologize beforehand to anyone offended by what is probably not a definition to everyone's liking.

As if this is not enough, I also sometimes throughout the book discuss various distances in the context of "a given caliber". It is important to make a definitional distinction between long absolute distance and long distance for a given caliber, defined as the distance in relation to the normal shooting range of a particular caliber. For example, while 200 meters or 218 yds is not a long distance for most rifle cartridges, it is an extremely long shooting distance for a .22 Long Rifle cartridge. Since the .22 LR has a low muzzle velocity and ballistic coefficient, at such distances it will be more affected by various external ballistic factors. For a .308 Winchester, on the other hand, 200 meters is not far at all and the trajectory is only marginally affected by many external ballistic factors. In this context, when I write "very long distance for a given caliber", I have in mind the end of the trajectory for that caliber, at which the projectile has lost a lot of its velocity and is more affected by various external ballistic factors. A short or medium range for a given caliber, on the other hand, would mean the early or middle portion of projectile's flight path, where it still retains a significant part of its initial velocity.

In a discussion about external ballistics, it is necessary to keep both of the above concepts in mind at the same time. In this book we will discuss different shooting distances both in an absolute sense, and also in a relative sense in regard to a specific cartridge or caliber.

BALLISTICS

Ballistics is the scientific study of thrown or fired projectiles. "Thrown or fired" is an important part of the definition, because it specifies that there is no constant propulsion of what is fired or thrown. Ballistics deals with projectiles that are propelled for some distance in flight, and then freely affected by the atmosphere: gravity, air resistance, air pressure, humidity, wind, etc. Thus, throwing rocks in a lake is as much ballistics as shooting at targets 1000 meters away, or the army firing artillery at targets 25 kilometers away.

Ballistics is in turn divided into four subgroups:

- Internal ballistics
- Transition ballistics
- External ballistics
- Terminal ballistics

Internal ballistics deals with what happens to the projectile in the weapon: ignition of the powder charge, expansion of the powder gases, propulsion of the bullet, the bullet's encounter with the lands in the barrel, and the bullet's travel through the barrel.

Transition ballistics deals with the short part of the projectile's journey when it transitions from being propelled by the high-pressure gases in the barrel to traveling freely in the air.

External ballistics is what this book is about - the projectile's flight through the air to the target. External ballistics includes such factors as gravity, air drag, wind drift, gyroscopic drift, the Coriolis effect, the Eötvös effect, and aerodynamic jump. In short, it deals with the relation between the projectile and the atmosphere on the way to the target.

Terminal ballistics is concerned with what happens with the bullet when it impacts the target, as well as inside the target. Terminal ballistics is very important, especially for hunters and for military research. Hunters tend to be very interested in how their bullets work inside game, and often have strong opinions about different makes and models of bullets. For military purposes, terminal ballistics is important because we want to be able to penetrate the enemy's armor and do enough damage to incapacitate them. For sport shooters, terminal ballistics is not the focus for obvious reasons. Sport shooters are usually more interested in external ballistics rather than terminal ballistics, as it does not matter how the bullet performs *after* hitting a target in competition.

RIFLE DISCIPLINES AND EXTERNAL BALLISTICS

This chapter reflects on how external ballistic factors manifest themselves in different rifle shooting disciplines. There are many different forms of rifle shooting, such as hunting (which itself is extremely broad with many different environments and calibers), air rifle (10 m), short range shooting (50 m) with .22lr, biathlon and field shooting with .22lr, 300 meters with caliber 6.5x55 mm, field shooting, PRS (*Precision Rifle Series*) at very long distances, F-class, dynamic shooting and many more. Since the Field Shooting discipline is not widely known outside the Scandinavian countries, I will briefly describe it here. Field shooting is a shooting event, popular in the Nordics, with deep military roots. The caliber is either 6.5 mm or 7.62 mm with bolt-action rifles, and the targets are distributed at unknown distances up to about 800 meters and sometimes beyond. The targets themselves are nowadays stylized shapes of enemy soldiers, with 1/3, half and full figure cardboard targets. The size of the targets is known beforehand, so by using the reticles of the rifle sights or scope the shooter approximates the distance to the target, and within a certain time period fires six shots. A field shooting competition has a number of shooting stations, with varying distances and target sizes. At the end of the competition, a final score is calculated for each shooter, and if two shooters have the same score an extra shooting station is used in order to determine the winner. This is a great way to learn to learn precision rifle shooting in applied form, and quite similar to real military situations. The same kind of competition also exists with .22 LR rifles, and the main benefit of this discipline is that competitions are much easier to arrange with the less powerful caliber.

Hunting and shooting sports are rich in disciplines, and these different disciplines involve different external ballistic considerations. There are many different aspects of external ballistic impact on projectiles. The table of contents of this book is a relatively exhaustive list of external ballistic aspects relevant to rifle shooting. However, *not all types of external ballistic effects are relevant to all kinds of shooting.* This may seem trivial to point out, but it needs to be said. The elk hunter standing 50 meters away from a bull moose does not need to care about the rotation of the Earth to judge where to aim the rifle. He does not even have to worry about the wind, unless it is so strong that it affects his own shooting technique. The basic rule for thinking about external ballistic effects is *the longer the distance, the more aspects of external ballistics are relevant.* Compare the competitive shooter at 300 meters with the military sniper, who has to engage a target at 1500 meters. The competitive shooter usually only needs to take into account the distance (the effect of gravity and air resistance) and the wind to make a hit. The sniper, on the other hand, must consider distance, angle of fire, wind, air temperature, air pressure, humidity, Coriolis effect, Eötvös effect, gyroscopic drift and possibly wind gradient (depending on the surrounding environment). As we can see from the example above, there is a considerable difference in difficulty as we extend the shooting distance. The example above is extreme, but I use it to illustrate that the external ballistic challenges increase with distance, not least because more variables have to be taken into account.

It would be possible to make a kind of graph or table for the distances at which different external ballistic influences become relevant, but it is usually not possible to say that a certain external ballistic phenomenon *only* becomes important after a certain distance. This would be an oversimplification. In reality, external ballistic effects are an interaction between weapon systems, ammunition performance and distance. This means that a faster and heavier bullet with a higher ballistic coefficient[1] will be significantly less affected by external ballistic phenomena at a certain distance, than a slower bullet with a lower ballistic coefficient. Thus, it is *not only* the distance that determines how difficult a particular shot is, but also what other components and variables are part of that shot. This also means that it is important to use the right weapon system and caliber, to make a particular shot. There are good reasons why a military force would not engage enemy troops at 1300 meters with a 6.5 mm caliber. Firstly, the impact energy would be too low to cause sufficient damage; secondly, the shot would involve so many, and so difficult, external ballistic considerations that it would be inappropriate. Instead, a larger caliber with a heavier bullet and better ballistic coefficient is chosen to make the shot. By doing this, we do not eliminate the external ballistic difficulties, but we reduce them and thereby increase our chances of hitting the target.

---

[1] The meaning of ballistic coefficient will be explained in detail below.

HUNTING OR SPORTS SHOOTING

Hunters and sport shooters often have different interests in ballistics. Most hunters are more interested in terminal ballistics than external ballistics, and for sport shooters it is often the other way around. This is not surprising, as we don't have to spend time thinking about how well a bullet penetrates a cardboard target or a steel plate. The main purpose of the shot is the hit itself, and not the nature of the hit. But as hunting distances are extended, the hunter's understanding of external ballistics becomes more important. Even a 200-meter shot at a deer can go wrong if we don't understand the effects of gravity, air resistance and wind on the bullet trajectory. The longer the distances, the more important the external ballistic considerations become. There is a well-developed discourse on hunting ethics and shooting distances, and that is not a debate I intend to get into here. We can only conclude that every hunter is responsible for his or her shots, and should not take a shot that he or she is not sure will kill the game quickly and effectively. Hopefully, through a deeper knowledge of external ballistics, hunters can become better shooters not only at long distances but also at normal hunting distances.

In theory, external ballistic effects are more important for hunting bullets than match (target) bullets. This is because match bullets are built to overcome external ballistic obstacles, while many hunting bullets are designed with primarily terminal ballistic considerations in focus. The result of this is that hunting bullets typically have poorer external ballistic properties than competition bullets. For example, a match bullet with a high ballistic coefficient is less affected by air resistance and wind drift[2] than a hunting bullet with a lower ballistic coefficient. In practice, however, more difficult external ballistic considerations are usually limited to sport shooting, as hunting is often done at such short distances that the hunter does not have to think too much about external ballistic factors.

This is not to say that all hunting bullets have a low ballistic coefficient. There are hunting bullets on the market that have as high a ballistic coefficient as match bullets of the same caliber. These bullets are designed primarily for places in the world where plains or mountainous terrain require longer hunting shots than in other places.

---

[2] The physical mechanism that causes wind drift is discussed in later chapters.

BALLISTIC COEFFICIENT (BC)

Ballistic coefficient, often abbreviated BC, is necessary to be familiar with for rifle shooters. BC is recurring in my examples and explanations, and therefore an explanation of the meaning of it is needed. For short hunting or shooting distances, the ballistic coefficient is not decisive when choosing a bullet. Ballistic coefficient becomes important only at higher precision requirements and longer distances, which is what the rest of this chapter will deal with.

The ballistic coefficient is typically explained as a measure of how well a projectile withstands air drag, or how well a projectile maintains its velocity through the air. A higher ballistic coefficient means that a certain projectile maintains its velocity better than one with a lower ballistic coefficient. But the common definitions of ballistic coefficient I have given above are not complete. Often a part of the definition of ballistic coefficient is omitted. The part left out is that ballistic coefficient is a measure of how well a projectile withstands air resistance compared to a reference (or standard) projectile. This standard projectile is important for understanding the differences between different ballistic coefficients.

The invention of the standard projectile was a very important discovery in modern exterior ballistics. It was the British priest and mathematician Francis Bashforth who developed the concept in 1865-1870, when working for the Royal Military Academy in Woolwich where he taught British artillery officers.[3] The idea of the

---

[3] McDonald, William T. and Almgren, Ted C. (2008)

standard projectile is to be able to calculate the external ballistic properties of any projectile, based on the known performance of a standard projectile, without having to perform extensive testing on the former. Basically, if we know the exact external ballistic behavior of a standard projectile, and we compare the properties of that standard projectile with a new projectile, we are able to calculate and anticipate the drag properties of the new projectile without ever having shot it. The standard projectile that Bashforth proposed was very similar to the G1 standard projectile that is still commonly used today.

The new method revolutionized the ballistics field, and promised to save both time and money when developing new projectiles, as well as comparing the ballistic properties of different projectiles. The idea of the standard projectile took root in the ballistics field, and was further developed during the work of the Gavre Commission in France, which existed from 1873 to 1898, and performed extensive testing on different projectiles. The tradition of naming standard projectiles with the letter G, such as G1 or G7, is in honor of the Gavre Commission.

There are two types of ballistic coefficients commonly used for rifle bullets: G1 and G7. The ballistic coefficient of a bullet is normally presented as follows: BC (G1): .410. "G1" indicates the reference (or standard) projectile used in the formula to calculate BC, and .410 is the actual value of the ballistic coefficient, which is normally expressed to three decimal places. The designations G1 or G7 in brackets are the names of reference projectiles to which the bullet in question is compared, when calculating its ballistic coefficient. The ballistic coefficient is fed into a ballistic calculator to model bullet trajectories. The values from that calculation are then used by the hunter or shooter to compensate for the effect of external ballistic factors on the bullet.

The rest of this chapter will be devoted to explaining the sources of error in the modeling of the bullet trajectory, due to the different reference projectiles. If you are not interested in understanding the underlying causes, it is sufficient to know that BC (G7) should be used in calculations when shooting at longer distances, as it gives a more accurate result compared to BC (G1).

What is important to understand is that the stated ballistic coefficient of a projectile is correct for a certain velocity, but is slightly incorrect for other velocities. This is because the formula for calculating the BC of a projectile contains a coefficient[4], known as the *form coefficient*, which is calculated for a specific velocity. When the projectile moves beyond that velocity, the given value for the projectile is more or less inaccurate. In reality, this margin of error is small, but when shooting at very long distances these variations can be important. A simplified way of expressing this is that BC is calculated at a certain velocity, and that BC is not completely accurate at other velocities. The variation in BC over velocity is real, and occurs because of changes in the air flow around the projectile at different velocities. This is explained further when discussing drag coefficient below.

If the BC has been calculated from a high velocity, i.e. at the beginning of the trajectory, the error for long range shooting will be greater than if the value has been calculated at a lower velocity. Manufacturers of bullets often do not indicate the velocity at which

---

[4] Coefficient is a multiplicative factor in a mathematical term.

they have calculated their ballistic coefficients, and it can therefore be difficult for consumers to know how well the bullets work at longer ranges. Recently, some manufacturers using G1 for shooting bullets have started to use a ballistic coefficient averaged over a certain distance of flight. This is better than using G1 calculated from shorter distances, as the ballistic coefficient tends to decrease with decreasing velocity. It is best for competitive shooting, especially at long distances, to always use BC (G7) if it is specified. The standard G1 projectile has much greater variation in its drag coefficient over different velocities than the G7 does, with the consequence that there is greater potential for error when using G1 as a reference projectile for modern rifle bullets. If we imagine shooting two projectiles that look like G1 and G7 at the same time next to each other, their trajectories are quite similar at the beginning when they are both at high velocity, in a standard hunting rifle about 800-900 m/s (2600-2950 fps). As the velocity drops to below 600 m/s or about 2000 fps later in the trajectory, the G1 projectile's drag coefficient increases faster than the G7 projectile. Thus, the G1 projectile starts to fly relatively poorly through the air after a while and the difference in the ability of the bullets to maintain velocity gets bigger and bigger the longer the trajectories are. A G7 projectile handles air resistance relatively well even after its velocity has decreased to 450 m/s or about 1500 fps, while the G1 projectile at this velocity begins to fall like a rock.

There is also an aspect of ballistic coefficient that concerns how ammunition and bullet manufacturers relate to ballistic coefficients. Since it is well known that a higher ballistic coefficient is generally considered to be better than a lower one, there is an incentive for manufacturers to market their bullets with a ballistic coefficient calculated for higher velocities, even though this value is less accurate at longer ranges. This also tends to be a fairly harmless trick on the part of manufacturers, since most hunting shots are made at relatively short distances. For the long-range shooter, however, this practice is annoying because it makes it harder to figure out how a bullet works at longer distances. It is a welcome trend that more and more manufacturers are starting to provide more information on how they have obtained their ballistic coefficients, in order to be more transparent. It is increasingly common for manufacturers to give different values calculated at different velocities, or to give an average value for a certain range of velocities. Such methods make it easier to get an idea of how good a bullet is at longer distances.

Another reason why BC (G1) is still the most common choice for a manufacturer is that BC (G1) gives a larger absolute value than BC (G7). For example, if we take a 6.5 mm caliber bullet with BC (G1): 548, then with BC (G7) it has a value of about 0.274, i.e. half the value of the BC (G1). There is some discussion that manufacturers are afraid to switch to BC (G7) because they would have to start printing a lower absolute value on their boxes of bullets and ammunition, which may lead some buyers to choose a box with a higher (G1) ballistic coefficient instead. Despite the arguments against switching to BC (G7), there is a tendency for bullet manufacturers to become more responsive to the needs of sport shooters and to publish more accurate ballistic information about their bullets so that shooters and hunters can make more informed purchases.

In summary, the BC (G7) should be used for long range competition shooting or long-range hunting. For shooting or hunting at short distances it does not matter very much which of the different types we choose. It is important to note that *a bullet with a higher ballistic coefficient not only experiences lower drag, but also less wind drift due to crosswind.* Exactly why a higher ballistic coefficient results in less wind drift will be explained in the chapter on wind drift below. There are thus clear advantages to using bullets with a high ballistic coefficient when shooting competitively or hunting at longer distances.

The future of the ballistic coefficient

Standard projectiles have been around for a long time and are likely to be around for a long time, but there are other proposals for systems to predict how bullets fly. For example, the American manufacturer Hornady has launched a ballistic calculator that uses the drag coefficient of bullets to calculate the bullet trajectory instead of going through a form coefficient. This approach is likely to be very accurate and give good results for long range shooting. The disadvantage is the extensive work, for the manufacturer, that must be done with radar to measure and calculate the exact drag coefficient of all bullets at different velocities. Not all manufacturers have the resources to do this.

Calculation of the ballistic coefficient

This section will discuss the methods used to calculate the ballistic coefficient. Below is the equation used to calculate the ballistic coefficient.

$$BC_{Projectile} = \frac{m/7000}{cal^2 \times i}$$

In which:

$BC_{Projectile}$ = the answer obtained from the equation in the unit of pounds per square inch. As a rule, the unit of measurement pounds per square inch is omitted and only the numerical value of the ballistic coefficient is shown. The actual unit that the value represents is also not very important, as the value is used to get a general idea of the aerodynamic properties of the bullet, or to compare with the ballistic coefficients of other projectiles.

m = mass of the bullet in the unit grain (gn). One grain = 0.0647989 grams.

cal = bullet caliber (diameter) in inches.

i = *form coefficient or form factor* which is a dimensionless value. The fact that the value is dimensionless means that it does not have a unit such as centimeters or meters. The form coefficient is itself the solution of a different equation.

Form coefficient

The form coefficient is calculated by comparing the drag coefficient of the projectile with the drag coefficient of a standard projectile, usually G1 or G7. The form coefficient is used in the calculation of the ballistic coefficient. The form coefficient is calculated using the following formula:

$$i = \frac{C_p}{C_G}$$

In which:

i = form coefficient or form factor.

C_p = drag coefficient of the projectile in question

C_G = drag coefficient of a standard projectile (for rifle shooting typically G1 or G7).

Standard projectiles

Figure 1: the standard projectile G1

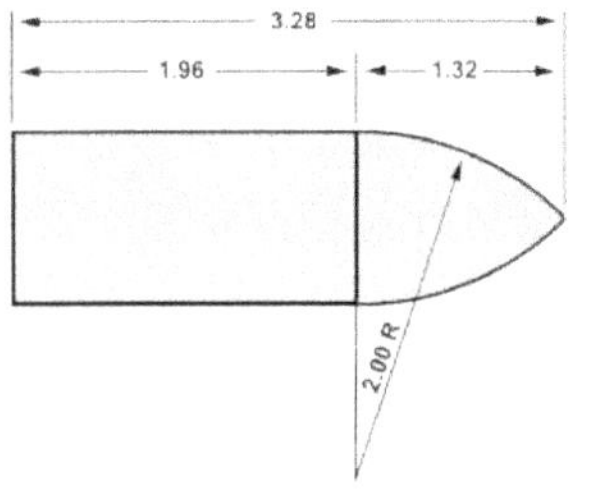

The G1 standard projectile looks more like an artillery projectile than a modern rifle competition bullet. The G1 model has survived to this day, and is still the most widely used model to compare bullets against. However, the G7 is becoming more commonly used for competition and long-range bullets.

---

[5] By Francis Flinch - Own work, CC BY-SA 3.0

Figure 2: the standard projectile G7

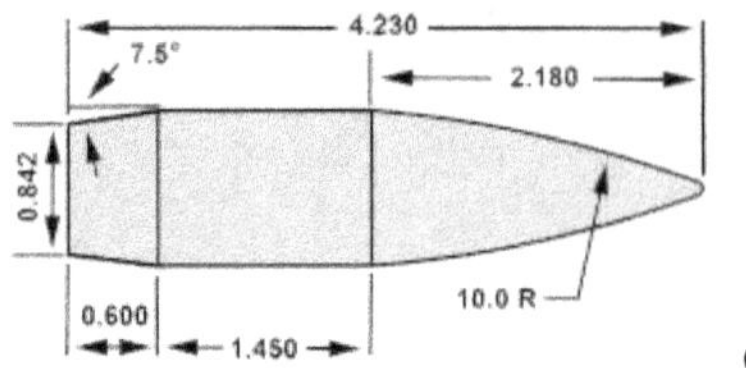

The G7 standard projectile was the result of research conducted by the British External Ballistics Department in the Ordnance Board of the War Office. The G7 standard projectile is much more similar to modern rifle bullets than the G1 standard projectile, which is basically the reason why the BC G7 value is more accurate for long range shooting than the BC G1.

Drag coefficient

As mentioned above, the drag coefficient of projectiles is used to calculate the form coefficient, which in turn is needed to calculate the ballistic coefficient. The drag coefficient is inversely related to the aerodynamic performance of the bullet. The higher the drag coefficient of a body, the more it is affected by drag and vice versa. Below is the formula to calculate the drag coefficient.

$$C_{drag} = \frac{2F_d}{pu^2 A}$$

---

[6] By Francis Flinch - Own work, CC BY-SA 3.0

In which:

C_{drag} = Drag coefficient

F_d = Drag Force

p = density of the fluid (air)

u = velocity of the projectile in relation to the fluid

A = the reference area of the projectile (area where the fluid meets the projectile)

The drag coefficient is calculated for a specific velocity, and the other calculations of BC are based on this, which means that BC is correct for one velocity. Since the G1 standard projectile exhibits greater variation than the G7 standard projectile in drag coefficient over velocity, this leads to a greater error when using the BC (G1) for longer range shooting. Manufacturers have traditionally given *one* value for their BC (G1), which is thus calculated based on coefficients for a specific velocity, often the velocity at 100 or 200 meters from the muzzle. When moving beyond that velocity, and especially at longer ranges towards the end of the trajectory, the indicated BC (G1) no longer corresponds well to the actual BC of modern shooting bullets. This means a greater error when shooting at long distances for a given caliber, when using a bullet with BC (G1) calculated at a higher velocity. It is important to note that the change in drag coefficient, and therefore the change in form factor as well as BC, is real and not a mathematical artifact. The change in drag coefficient occurs because of relative internal movement in the boundary layer around the projectile as it moves through the air at different velocities.

Other standard projectiles

The G1 and G7 standard projectiles are by far the most common ones for rifle shooting, and G1 is still dominant. There are, however, other standard projectiles for other purposes. In his book, *Modern Exterior Ballistics: The Launch and Flight Dynamics of Symmetric Projectiles*, Robert L. McCoy devotes a section to explaining the history of some of the other G-model standard projectiles that exist. Some of these projectiles are today outdated, while others are still useful for modeling trajectories. The G1 to G6 models were extensively researched at the US military research and test site Aberdeen proving ground, while the G7 and G8 models were the results of research conducted by the British External Ballistics Department in the Ordnance Board of the War Office. Both the G7 and G8 standard projectiles are of a more streamlined design than the earlier models, but the G7 has a boat-tail while the G8 has a flat base. Both the G7 and G8 standard projectiles were extensively used during the Second World War to prepare ballistics tables, according to McCoy. The G8 standard projectile is very similar in its design to flat-base bullets used in bench-rest shooting. In bench-rest shooting, flat-base bullets are commonly used for shooting at short and medium distances. Flat-based projectiles have slightly different transitional ballistic properties than boat-tail projectiles, and tend to be more stable when transitioning from interior to exterior ballistics. Resistance to wind drift is, however, generally better in boat-tail projectiles than flat-base projectiles due to a higher ballistic coefficient.

BALLISTIC CALCULATORS

Modern ballistic calculators are very good at calculating bullet trajectories. Most ballistic calculators on the market, both free and premium, are basically very accurate programs that work well for rifle shooting at most distances. In addition, those that cost money are not always better than those that are free, which complicates matters. Most free programs offered by manufacturers are very similar to each other and produce similar results. However, some ballistic calculators are more advanced, and they can also include hard-to-access radar data from manufacturers. Such products include ballistic calculators from Dexadine, Lapua and Hornady. I personally mostly use the premium program Ballistic Explorer from Dexadine Inc., because it is one of the most comprehensive and easy to use programs on the market. I have no affiliation with them; I simply think it's a great product for high-level and professional users. For casual users, hunters and sport shooters it is possibly overkill, and many simpler programs will accomplish the job for most users. The Ballistic Explorer requires a fair amount of ballistic knowledge of the user to be used effectively. It is also a desktop program, which probably disqualifies it for many users, who tend to want a mobile phone application that they can bring to the range. Lapua also has a very competent ballistic calculator for small caliber cartridges at the moment, especially when we use Lapua's projectiles for which they have collected extensive data. One good open-source ballistic calculator is JBM ballistics, which will satisfy the needs of most users. Since I use ballistic calculators, including those from Dexadine and Lapua, to calculate many of the examples in this book, it is necessary to spend some time discussing ballistic calculators and the physics behind them, before moving on to external ballistics.

Degrees of freedom

As mentioned above, most ballistic programs on the market are very similar to each other and give similar results. This is basically because they solve the *same mathematical problems* for calculating projectile trajectories, but they can solve these problems in slightly different ways. This chapter briefly describes how ballistic calculators calculate bullet trajectories, but to understand ballistic calculators we need to start with some basic physics.

In physics, *six degrees of freedom* are needed to accurately describe the position of a rigid body, in this case a projectile, in space. Degrees of Freedom are abbreviated DOF in ballistic contexts. Often when looking at ballistic applications on the web, we see terms like 3DOF, 4DOF or 6DOF. We will find out in this chapter what this actually means, and what significance it has for ballistic calculators.

There are primarily two types of motion that are of interest to external ballistics: *translation* and *rotation*. Translational degrees of freedom, also known as linear degrees of freedom, describe the movement of a projectile from one place to another in space. Rotational degrees of freedom do not describe movement from one place to another, but rotation.

Figure 3: Linear degrees of freedom

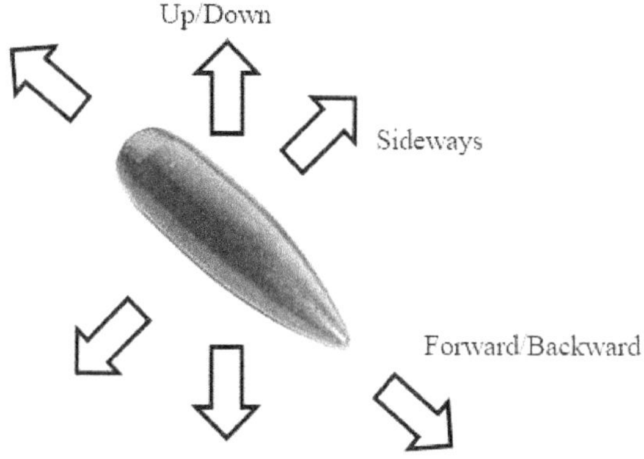

Figure 4: Rotational degrees of freedom

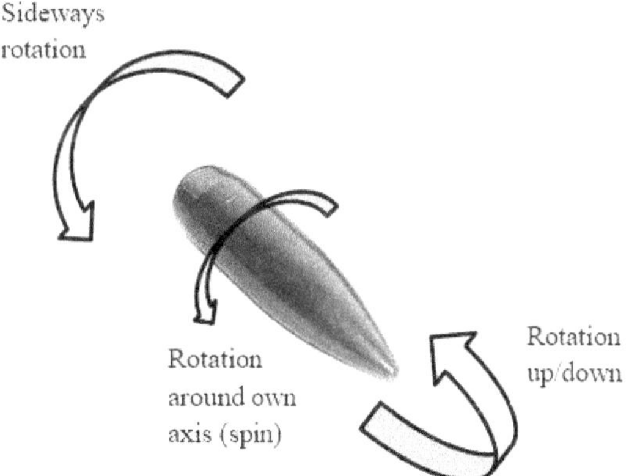

The rotation from side to side is called *yaw* and the up/down rotation is called *pitch*. When we combine all six types of degrees of freedom, we can accurately describe the position of a rigid body in space. If we remove any of the degrees of freedom, we can no longer describe the location and position of the body with the same precision. A ballistic calculator that considers more degrees of freedom in its calculations has the potential to provide more accurate results than one that uses fewer degrees of freedom. However, this assumes that the values entered into the equations are correct, and that the mathematical problems have been solved correctly.

Three degrees of freedom

The vast majority of ballistic calculators for small arms use only the translational degrees of freedom, and not the rotational degrees of freedom, to calculate bullet trajectories. This means considering the bullet as a point in the air that cannot rotate, but only move linearly forward, up or down, and sideways. This method of calculating bullet trajectories is often referred to as the *Point Mass Method* (*PMM*). This is of course a simplification of how a projectile actually moves. Rifle projectiles rotate in different ways during flight, which will be discussed in detail in later chapters. Thus, in order to predict the trajectory of a projectile as accurately as possible, it is necessary to take into account all the degrees of freedom and not just the linear ones. The ballistic calculators that do not take into account rotation in different axes cannot achieve as high a theoretical accuracy as a 6DOF ballistic calculator. However, *they are usually good enough for most users' purposes.* They are typically sufficient for rifle shooting at a 1000 meters or yards and even longer, which is significantly longer than most people ever shoot a rifle. The fact that most ballistic calculators do not fully take the movement of the projectile in account does not mean that they are bad, but that they are considered sufficient for a particular purpose. There are also variants of ballistic calculators called 4DOF, which take into account some form of rotation in addition to the three degrees of freedom of translation. These ballistic calculators typically include yaw, which leads to a more accurate prediction of gyroscopic drift, since gyroscopic drift depends on the *yaw angle* of the bullet, as discussed in later chapters.

Six degrees of freedom

As noted above, we need all six degrees of freedom to accurately describe the position of a rigid body in space, and ballistic calculators that do this are generally considered more accurate than those that do not. Another reason why not all calculators use six degrees of freedom, except that three degrees of freedom is good enough for most, is that we need much more data about a projectile to be able to calculate six degrees of freedom. Until relatively recently this data was something that not even the manufacturers themselves had about their projectiles. This has changed, as bullet manufacturers now often have advanced radars that can record the exact characteristics of a particular bullet in flight. Based on such measurements, it is then possible to calculate various values needed to predict a bullet trajectory accurately at very long distances. The Finnish ammunition manufacturer Lapua was, to my knowledge, the first to map its bullets this accurately and to offer a public ballistic calculator that can use this data. For this reason, among others, Lapua's bullets are very popular with long-range shooters. The American companies Berger Bullets and Hornady are two other companies that are very advanced in regard to ballistic data about their products. At this point there are probably other manufacturers that are catching up, eager to get in on the precision long-range shooting market.

Despite the emergence of advanced 6DOF ballistic calculators on the civilian market, it is still primarily military forces that use six degrees of freedom for artillery and ballistic missiles. Artillery is used at much longer distances than rifle shooting, which is one reason why they need more advanced ballistic calculators. Since inaccuracies in calculating projectile trajectories increase with distance, better ballistic calculators and more accurate data are required the longer the trajectory is. However, the technology to record and calculate this data has become more available, which is one of the reasons why manufacturers can provide detailed data on their projectiles.

The calculations

It is impossible to determine with a single calculation exactly what a particular trajectory will look like. This is because the calculation of trajectories involves non-linear variables. The fact that a variable is non-linear means that it cannot be described graphically by a straight line. An example of such a variable in external ballistics is the drag coefficient. The drag coefficient is not constant throughout the trajectory but, as mentioned in the previous chapter, changes depending on the velocity of the projectile. Since the velocity of the projectile decreases dramatically during the trajectory, this needs to be accounted for in the calculation for it to be correct. The non-linear behavior of bullet trajectories means that we need to use *numerical methods* to calculate bullet trajectories. This basically means breaking down the trajectory into smaller parts to see how each small part relates to the next part of the trajectory.

Mathematically, one differential equation[7] is needed for each degree of freedom to calculate a ballistic trajectory. So, for ballistic calculators with three degrees of freedom, three differential equations are used, and for six degrees of freedom three more differential equations are needed. Unfortunately, a ballistic solution based on six degrees of freedom is not only twice as complex as one based on three degrees of freedom. Instead, it is several times more complex and also requires many more types of coefficients in order to perform the calculations. Collecting and calculating the necessary data is time-consuming, costly, and can hardly be done by a private individual.

The differential equations for calculating ballistic trajectories have been known since long before we had satisfactory means to solve them. Most ballistic calculators on the market solve three differential equations for the translational degrees of freedom, plus possibly an equation for a rotational degree of freedom, by plotting a graph of the ballistic trajectory. However, as noted above, there is no perfect solution to these differential equations, and some kind of numerical iterative method must be used to obtain an approximation of the motion of the projectile. The fact that the method is iterative means that it is repetitive. In practice, this is done by calculating a small part of the bullet path, and then using values from the previous calculation to advance the bullet path to the next step. In this way, a ballistic calculator "steps" through a bullet trajectory to reach the end point. Thus, using an iterative numerical method circumvents

---

[7] A differential equation is an equation that describes a relationship between a function and its derivative.

the problem that a ballistic trajectory is non-linear and cannot be solved by a single calculation.

This is where different ballistic calculators may differ slightly: they may use different numerical methods to solve the same differential equations, and they can divide the ballistic trajectory in different ways. There are several methods for solving differential equations by step methods, and there are also other ways in which ballistic calculators can differ: some step through the bullet path in absolute length, i.e. meters, yards and so on, while others step through the time of flight, e.g. hundredths of a second. They may also differ in the step length through the trajectory. This step length is not fixed but can be chosen by the mathematician who designs the ballistic calculator. Some ballistic calculators use fixed step lengths, such as one meter, to step through a bullet path while others use a dynamic method that changes the step length depending on the length of the bullet path. All of the above details produce slight differences in the results, which is why different ballistic calculators can display different projectile trajectories. There are decidedly ballistic calculators that are better than others, but for most users, in most cases, we will not notice much difference in practical application.

Ballistic calculators based on three degrees of freedom provide sufficient accuracy for rifle shooters in most cases. Possible exceptions are shooters who compete in precision shooting at ranges well over 1000 meters/1100 yards. At such distances, the difference between a 3DOF ballistic calculator and a 6DOF can be noticeable.

Thus, ballistic calculators do not provide a perfect picture of a bullet trajectory, but are only an approximation of what the bullet trajectory looks like. There is always a small margin of error. But these methods have evolved to the point where, although not perfect in a mathematical sense, they are very close representations of the actual trajectory. They are so good that it is usually not the calculator that is the problem when we don't hit what we want. Instead, it is usually we who have either entered some incorrect values into the calculator, or have some systematic shooting error such as shooting position, breathing, aiming, or firing, that causes us to miss. There is a common saying about ballistic calculators that goes "GIGO" or "garbage in, garbage out". This of course means that we can never get accurate results from a ballistic calculator if we feed it incorrect information. For example, if a shooter enters a muzzle velocity that is seven m/s (22 fps) wrong and an air temperature that is 10° C wrong, this will result in a significant error at longer distances. It is easier to blame the ballistic calculator than to verify our own data. Before switching from one ballistic calculator to another, it would be wise to check our own data to make sure we have not made a mistake. We should also not forget that measured values can change, so that previously correct ballistic calculations become incorrect, for example at a different time of year. Take the temperature stability of gunpowder as an example. If we measure the muzzle velocity of the ammunition in the summer, and then shoot a competition in the late fall, it would be wise to measure the muzzle velocity again to make sure it has not changed too much. If we don't, we may be in for an unpleasant surprise in competition when we don't hit where we want to.

THE RIFLE BULLET

There are many different types of rifle bullets. Of interest to external ballistics is what is commonly referred to as *bullet design* and *bullet construction*. The concept of bullet design includes the characteristics of the bullet that dictate its external ballistic properties. Among these characteristics are external shape (profile), diameter, length and weight. Bullet construction refers to aspects such as the choice of materials, how the different parts of the bullet are joined, the thickness of the jacket and any expansion mechanism. Bullet construction is primarily important for the terminal ballistic properties of a bullet, but can also be of interest for the external ballistics. For example, a bullet may have irregularities in the jacket or core that affect its external ballistic properties. There are also bullets that have the same material in the jacket and core. Such bullets are called *monolithic* and are becoming increasingly common, mainly in hunting but also in shooting at very long distances. They are becoming more common in hunting because they are usually lead-free, and it is positive that they do not leave toxic lead residues in the game or in nature. In shooting, they are mostly used in competition shooting at very long distances, in larger calibers, usually over .4 inches (10 mm). These bullets are often produced in small batches on computerized lathes and can achieve very tight tolerances as well as extremely high ballistic coefficients. Monolithic bullets for competitive shooting are therefore very expensive.

A brief history of rifle bullets

Rifled barrels were invented as early as the late 15th century in Germany, but due to their more expensive and difficult production, it took several hundred years for them to finally become widespread in the 19th century. Before rifled barrels became standard, the round ball was the dominant type of projectile. The round ball was originally shot in smoothbore barrels, i.e., barrels that do not have grooves and lands like modern rifle barrels. Obviously, a round ball has a symmetrical design, and regardless of which part of the bullet meets the air resistance, it has the same external ballistic properties. This means that the round ball does not need to be rotated to stabilize it, but it is predictable in flight anyway. However, the cast bullets of the time were not always very round, and the bullets could have imbalances and flaws in the surface that negatively affected their external ballistic properties. But the lack of precision of smoothbore muskets cannot be blamed solely on the rounds. Since the black powder of the time was very impure and created deposits in the barrel, the bullets had to be cast smaller than the caliber to make it easier to reload after a few shots. Since the bullets were smaller in diameter than the barrel, there was some unpredictability in accuracy, as the bullets could leave the barrel in a slightly different direction with each shot. Another problem with the muskets was that the amount of powder poured into the barrel differed slightly between each shot. This was due to the fact that the shooter put some of the powder from the cartridge, which consisted of a paper sleeve filled with powder and a round ball, into the pan that would ignite the main charge. The remaining powder was poured into the barrel, which resulted in the amount of powder in the barrel varying between each shot. This contributed to what could be a quite significant spread in the muzzle velocity of the round ball.

Paradoxically, the poor range and accuracy of the smoothbore muskets was not a major problem, because the black powder used in repeated firing created a black smoke that settled over the battlefield, making it difficult to see beyond a few tens of meters. As a result, fighting distances with muskets were often very short, and the weapons did not need a high degree of accuracy to hit an enemy soldier. However, muskets were not always reliable and the exposed powder was sensitive to rain and high humidity. Later, different materials were used to seal the space between the round ball and the larger diameter barrel. This material could be wool or felt, and partially solved the problem of the bullet leaving the muzzle in slightly different directions. However, loading became more difficult and more force was required to push the bullet and the wad into a dirty barrel.

Bullets were usually cast from lead. Lead is suitable for the core of bullets because of its high weight, which means that the bullet in flight has high kinetic energy, and it is therefore more difficult to stop or to change its direction. Lead is also a common element, and has a low melting point, meaning that shooters could melt lead and cast bullets themselves without having to buy the services of a blacksmith.

The first rifles were muzzle-loading muskets and also used round balls as projectiles. These were difficult to load, however, as the round ball was deformed as it was pushed down the barrel, and considerable force was required to load them. They were more accurate than smoothbore muskets but took longer to load. This changed with the invention of the so-called Minié ball by French army officer Claude-Étienne Minié in the 1840s, based on earlier work by his compatriots. The Minié ball was not a round ball, but one of the first modern bullets adapted for a rifled barrel. It was cast from lead and had a skirt at the base which, when fired, expanded and engaged the rifling in the barrel. Because the bullet expanded only during firing, it could be made smaller than the caliber of the barrel, and therefore as easy to load as a round ball in a smoothbore barrel. This development led to the replacement of smoothbore guns by rifled guns in the 19th century.

As the velocity of rifle bullets increased, it became increasingly difficult to use lead as the sole material in projectiles. Lead is a soft metal, and at higher muzzle velocities the pressure and friction in the barrel causes the lead bullet to leave significant deposits, in effect changing the diameter of the barrel and causing constrictions. In order to be able to fire projectiles longer, at higher velocity, the bullet had to be harder and not leave so much deposit in the barrel. However, it could not be so hard that the rifling could not deform it and force it to rotate. The problem was solved by splitting the bullet into two parts, starting in the 1880s, with a lead core and a copper jacket. The core is heavier and contributes a high kinetic energy; the copper is harder than the lead and can withstand higher muzzle velocities without leaving too much deposit in the barrel. This type of bullet is basically a modern rifle bullet, and it is small changes in materials and big changes in production technology that distinguish them from those that are fired today. Modern rifle bullets with a lead core do not have a jacket of pure copper but of tombac. Tombac is a collective name for brass alloys with a copper content of more than 70%. The jacket of ammunition is usually 95% copper and 5% zinc, but this can vary between manufacturers. Monolithic hunting bullets are typically also made of tombac. Since a tombac monolithic bullet is lighter than an equivalent lead core bullet of the same caliber, the monolithic bullet needs to be longer to achieve the same kinetic energy for a given velocity.

Different types of rifle bullets

Figure 5: Jacketed bullet

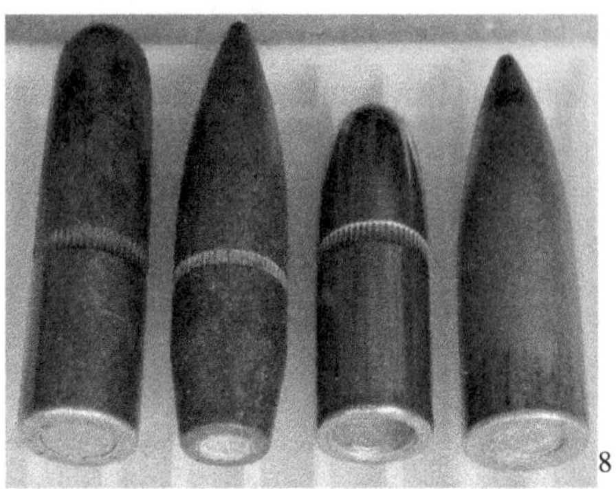

The fully jacketed bullet (usually called full metal jacket or FMJ) has a lead core and a jacket that completely covers the core at the tip. The full metal jacket bullet is not designed to expand in the target. Full metal jacket bullets are used for example in hunting small game and birds, as an expanding bullet would destroy too much of the meat. FMJ bullets are also used in warfare, originally based on the St. Petersburg Declaration of 1868, and then on the Hague Declaration of 1899, which concluded that semi-jacketed bullets should be banned in warfare, as they had the potential to cause particularly great harm in humans. This ban has been largely upheld by belligerent states. However, there is no obvious advantage for military forces to use semi-jacketed munitions, as they would have more difficulty penetrating modern body armor than full metal jacket bullets. When the Hague Declaration was written, soldiers did not wear body armor on the battlefield. In addition, modern full

---

[8] Thewellman, CC0, via Wikimedia Commons

metal jacket bullets often have a similar effect on the body as semi-jacketed bullets, as they travel very fast and can rotate or break apart, causing significant tissue damage in a human body.

Figure 6: Hollow point bullet

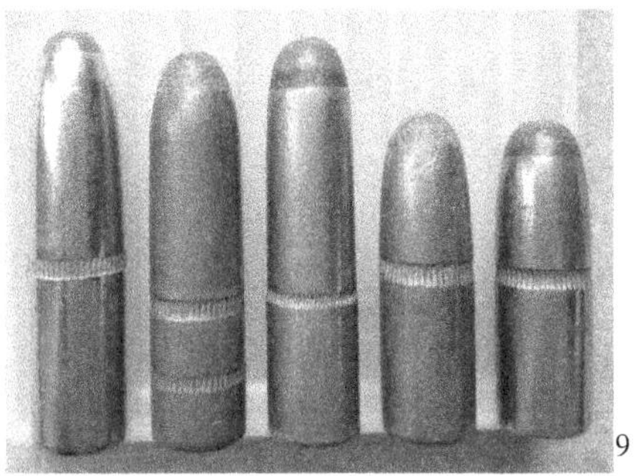

A semi-jacketed bullet has an opening in the jacket where the lead core is exposed. The hollow-point bullet is designed to expand in the target, thus increasing its diameter. The idea behind this is that a larger diameter projectile does more tissue damage to the target than a smaller diameter bullet. The sharp edges formed by an expanding bullet cut tissue better than a smooth bullet. A hollow-point bullet also reduces the risk of the bullet passing through the game and injuring someone behind the intended target. Of course, every hunter should see to it that there is some kind of bullet trap behind his target, but the risk of ricochet still exists. Many police forces around the world also use hollow point ammunition in their service weapons. This reduces the risk of a bullet passing through the target and hitting a third party. Hollow point bullets typically do not have a very high ballistic coefficient. This is because they are designed

---

[9] Thewellman, CC0, via Wikimedia Commons

for hunting, which in most cases takes place at short distances, where ballistic coefficient does not matter as much.

Figure 7: Semi-jacketed bullet with plastic tip

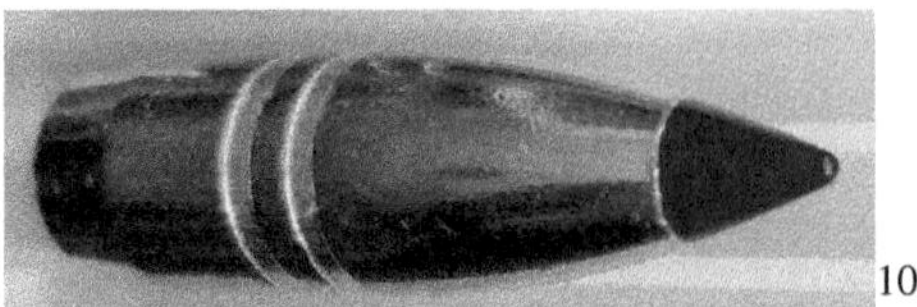

Hollow-point plastic-tipped bullets are a relatively recent invention, combining the expansion of the hollow point bullet with the higher ballistic coefficient of the full metal jacket bullet. Plastic-tipped bullets are usually marketed to hunters who hunt at long distances, such as in mountainous environments, and who may need bullets with a particularly high ballistic coefficient. An advantage of such bullets is that they can be used for both hunting and competitive shooting, which can offer an economic advantage as well as a practical one, as only one projectile's ballistic data needs to be managed for both hunting and target shooting.

Figure 8: Monolithic bullet for hunting

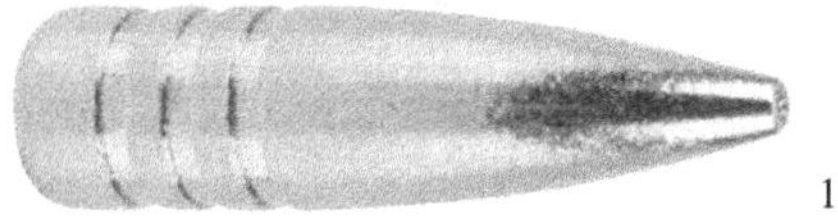

Monolithic bullets are not really a novelty, as even old round lead balls are in the technical sense monolithic. Nowadays, the term

---

[10] Thewellman, CC0, via Wikimedia Commons
[11] Author's image

monolithic is usually used for either hunting bullets or advanced match bullets. Monolithic hunting bullets, usually made entirely of tombac, have become more common due to an ambition to reduce the use of lead in hunting. As monolithic hunting bullets do not contain lead, they are safer both for humans who will eat the meat, as well as for the animals that eat the remains of animals in the wild. Because monolithic hunting bullets do not have a lead core, they need to be longer in a given caliber to achieve the same weight as a bullet with a lead core. This extra length means that the bullet has more surface area in contact with the rifling in the barrel, which in turn increases the friction in the barrel, and also the pressure in the gun. To reduce friction and pressure, grooves are often cut into the bullet, reducing the total surface area in contact with the rifling. Material scraped off by the rifling in the barrel may also be deposited in these grooves, reducing friction and deposits in the barrel.

Figure 9: Monolithic bullet for sport shooting

[12]

Another variant of monolithic projectiles is precision bullets produced on computerized lathes. The weight and other parameters of such a bullet can be controlled with extreme precision, resulting in bullets with very high uniformity. These bullets are very expensive and are used for precision shooting at very long distances. Monolithic match bullets are usually made from brass alloy, with

---

[12] Author's image

around 95% copper, but can also be made from pure copper. Monolithic match bullets in larger calibers, such as .375 inch (9.5 mm), can be used for shooting up to and 3000 meters and beyond, which places extremely high demands on the uniformity and quality of the bullet. For example, the most expensive monolithic projectiles are made only from new copper, and not recycled, in order to avoid contamination from other metals.

Figure 10: Open Tip Match (OTM)

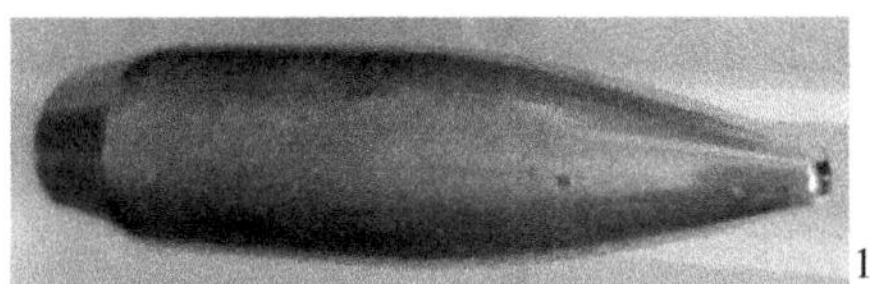13

OTM bullets are, as the name suggests, usually match bullets made for competitive shooting. The reason the tip is open is that the molten lead is poured into the bullet through the hole, allowing the weight of the core to be relatively well controlled. Modern OTM bullets are often well made and have great precision potential. OTM bullets are one of the most common types of competition bullets for long range precision shooting. There is some debate about whether the OTM bullet is semi-jacketed or fully jacketed. From a design point of view, the bullet has more in common with a fully jacketed bullet than a semi-jacketed one. The hole in the tip is a result of the manufacturing process, and is not an expansion mechanism designed to increase the diameter of the bullet as is the case with semi-jacketed bullets. OTM bullets are not as exclusive, nor have the same uniformity, as monolithic bullets produced in precision lathes. However, they are often perfectly adequate for shooting at

---

[13] Author's image

very long distances, well over 1000 meters, without being a limiting factor.

AIR

All discussions about external ballistics in one way or another concerns the relation between a fired projectile and air. For this reason, I believe it's prudent to briefly discuss the basic physical properties of air, before moving on to more advanced ballistic questions.

In a chemical sense, air consists mainly of nitrogen (78%) and oxygen (21%), with a small number of other gases such as argon, carbon dioxide and neon. There is also always a small and variable amount of water vapor in the air, which we will return to in the section on humidity. Air weighs about 1.3 kg per cubic meter (2.16 lbs. per cubic yard), although this varies with air density. The scientific study of air and air movement is called *fluid mechanics*. Just as we discuss how water moves and flows, we research how air flows and how turbulence in air currents occurs. Normally, when we are out walking in the outdoors, we don't think about the fact that the air is flowing around us in a similar way as water would if we were surrounded by water instead. It is often easier to understand air and wind for rifle shooting applications, if we get used to thinking of air as a liquid that flows through the terrain.

Air density

The density of air can vary. Air density is defined as the mass of air within a given volume. A higher density means that more molecules are contained within the same volume of air, and that volume therefore weighs more. When the air has a higher density, it is more difficult for a projectile to travel through it. The projectile experiences more air resistance (drag), and the projectile therefore loses velocity more quickly. When the air has a lower density, it is easier for the projectile to travel through it and maintains its velocity better. Thus, a bullet loses velocity faster in higher density air and slower in lower density air.

Atmospheric pressure

Atmospheric pressure is a concept directly related to air density. Atmospheric pressure is defined as the downward pressure exerted by the atmosphere on the Earth within a given area at a given time. Atmospheric pressure is greatest near the Earth's surface, because the entire weight of the atmosphere above that point rests on the Earth's surface. The higher up in the atmosphere, the lower the air pressure becomes because there is less and less air above that point exerting downward pressure. The weight of the air depends on the density of the air. The higher the density of the air, the greater the weight per unit of volume pushing against the Earth, and the greater the air pressure at the Earth's surface. So, there is a direct relationship between air density and pressure; as air density increases so does the air pressure.

Air temperature

When air becomes warmer, the molecules move faster and need more space. The molecules spread out, and there are fewer molecules within a given volume of air: the air becomes less dense. On the contrary, colder molecules do not move as much as warmer ones and the air is compressed more, giving it a higher density. Air temperature and atmospheric pressure thus have an inverse relationship: when the temperature of the atmosphere increases, the atmospheric pressure decreases; when the temperature of the atmosphere decreases, the atmospheric pressure increases.

Atmospheric pressure should not be confused with absolute pressure, because the physical rules and mechanisms governing the two are different. In a closed container, the air pressure will increase when the temperature of the air inside increases. The molecules have nowhere to go and are stuck in the container. As the molecules in the container heat up, they move more and the pressure in the container increases. In this case, there is a positive correlation between temperature and pressure: as the temperature increases, so does the pressure. This is not the case in the atmosphere, because the air in the atmosphere is not confined to a region of constant temperature, but is constantly moving between regions of different temperatures. This means that atmospheric pressure can vary within the same area, but generally stays within a certain range.

Unfortunately, it is not as simple as the altitude and air temperature being the only variables to determine atmospheric pressure, as global weather patterns come into play and have an impact. The uneven heating of the Earth by the sun's thermal radiation, together with the Earth's rotation and the Coriolis force, which we will come back to later, create temporary and semi-permanent areas of high and low pressure that affect the overall air pressure. A general rule is that air pressure in a given area is lower in summer than in winter, because the air temperature is higher. Warmer air also holds more water vapor, which in turn decreases the mass of the air, and also contributes to lower air pressure in warmer temperatures. Humidity will be discussed in more detail below.

Air drag

Air resistance, or drag, increases proportionally to the cross-sectional area of a projectile, but it increases with the square of the velocity of the projectile. This means that if you double the speed, the drag force will increase by a factor of four (assuming other factors remain constant). Thus, it becomes increasingly difficult for a projectile to increase its velocity the faster it flies. This is because as the projectile flies faster, it not only collides with more particles in flight, causing increased surface friction, but these particles also slow the projectile down relatively more, as the collision occurs at a higher velocity. A bullet fired from a rifle has the highest velocity just as it leaves the barrel, but starts to slow down immediately due to air drag. The projectile velocity decreases faster in the beginning of the bullet's trajectory, when the projectile is traveling at its greatest velocity.

Below is the drag formula.

$$D = \frac{1}{2}\rho V^2 C_d A$$

In which:

D = drag force

ρ = density of the fluid (air).

V = speed of the fluid in relation to the projectile

C_d = drag coefficient

A = cross-sectional area of the projectile

The impact of air temperature

The air temperature affects our shooting in primarily two ways, one of which concerns external ballistics and the other internal ballistics: air density and powder charge efficiency. There is also a third impact mechanism: the temperature's impact on the shooter. However, how cold and heat affect the shooter's ability is not something I intend to cover here; I leave that to your common sense. This book deals primarily with external ballistics, but since muzzle velocity is important to bullet performance, a brief discussion of temperature and powder charge efficiency is required.

Internal ballistic impact

The effect of temperature on gunpowder varies greatly between different gunpowders, but in general the muzzle velocity tends to increase with increasing temperature. A traditional rule of thumb is that for every 11° C that the temperature of the ammunition changes, the point of impact changes by 0.5-1 minute of angle (MOA)[14] (Angular measurements such as minute of angle and milliradian are explained in a later chapter). One minute of angle is equivalent to about 2.7 cm at 100 meters. However, anyone interested in precision shooting should make their own measurements and tables and not rely on rules of thumb. Some powders are more temperature-stable, while other powders can vary greatly in different temperatures. Gunpowders also tend to become more reliable and consistent over time, and a rule of thumb that was good 50 years ago may not be

---

[14] Angular measurements such as minute of angle and milliradian are explained in a later chapter.

today. In the past when hunters went to Africa to hunt with older gunpowder and large caliber big-game rifles, they often had to decrease the powder charge in the cartridges so that they would not achieve dangerously high pressures in their guns due to the heat.

For a long-range shooter, however, it is necessary to test-fire the weapons in the temperatures in which they are intended to be used. We should not rely on general rules, but go out to the shooting range in different temperatures with a chronograph to test shoot and document the data carefully. My own gunpowder from the Swedish manufacturer Norma has a variation in muzzle velocity of about 0.8-1 m/s (1.8-2.2 mph) per degree Celsius. It is of course desirable to have as good temperature stability as possible, but the most important thing is to *know how changes in temperature affect the muzzle velocity*. If there is a known change in muzzle velocity, it can be calculated and compensated for, thereby eliminating the issue. In precision shooting, repeatability and consistency is everything. There are certainly powders that are considered to be very temperature stable, and if we are trying to avoid the problem altogether, we should look for them. It is always good, however, to carry out our own tests to check the temperature stability and not blindly rely on the manufacturers' data.

External ballistic impact

The second way in which temperature affects shooting has to do with external ballistics, and the density of the air. A projectile encounters more air resistance traveling through cold air than warm air, because cold air is denser than warm air. There are more molecules, and therefore more mass, within a given volume of air that must be pushed aside as the bullet passes through. In general, it can be said that air temperature has a marginal effect on short to medium distances for a given caliber, but a potentially large effect on long and very long distances for a given caliber. Thus, when shooting at long distances for a given caliber, we may want to take into account the temperature of the air to hit the target. For example, one may want to consider air temperature as a separate variable when shooting a 6.5 mm rifle above 600-800 meters, when the rifle has been sighted in at a temperature that is significantly higher or lower than the present temperature. The longer the shooting range, and the more the present air temperature differs from the air temperature at which the rifle was sighted in, the more important it becomes to consider air temperature. For a hunter, hunting at short to medium distances, air temperature is hardly a variable that needs to be considered in terms of external ballistic impact on the trajectory.

The ballistic coefficient of the projectile also plays an important role in this context. This is not surprising because, as we have seen, the ballistic coefficient is a measure of a projectile's ability to overcome the air resistance. It doesn't matter what the density of the air is at the moment: a bullet with a higher ballistic coefficient experiences less bullet drop than a bullet with a lower ballistic coefficient in a given caliber. We will look at some examples to illustrate how air temperature affects the trajectories of different rifle calibers. We start by looking at a couple of common calibers: 6.5x55 mm, 6.5 Creedmoor and .308 Winchester, and then at a caliber for shooting at longer distances, .338 Lapua Magnum. The values in the table in centimeter/inches is the absolute bullet drop from the rifle bore axis. The muzzle velocity in the calculations below is constant for all temperatures, so the varying powder charge efficiency at different temperatures does not affect the results. The air temperature is the only variable that changes in the examples.

Impact of air temperature on bullet trajectory

Table 1: 6.5x55 mm (metric)

- 130 gn (8.42 grams) match bullet
- BC (G7): 0.274
- 900 m/s (2950 fps) muzzle velocity
- Relative humidity 40 %
- Air pressure 1015 hPa

		Distance (m)						
		100	200	300	400	500	600	700
T	30	6.3	26.4	62.3	116.2	190	289	416
E	20	6.3	26.5	62.5	116.7	192	291	419
M	10	6.3	26.6	62.8	117.4	193	294	424
P	0	6.3	26.6	63	118.1	195	297	429
(C)	- 10	6.4	26.7	63.3	118.9	196	300	435
	- 20	6.4	26.8	63.7	119.7	198	303	441

Absolute bullet drop (cm)

Table 2: 6.5x55 mm (imperial)

Table 2 is based on the same parameters as table 1 above.

		Distance (yd)						
		100	200	300	400	500	600	700
T	86	2.1	8.6	20.3	37.7	61.7	92	133
E	68	2.1	8.6	20.4	37.8	62	93	134
M	50	2.1	8.7	20.4	38	62.3	94	135
P	32	2.1	8.7	20.5	38.2	62.7	95	136
(F)	14	2.1	8.7	20.6	38.4	63.2	95	138
	-4	2.1	8.7	20.7	38.6	63.7	96	140

Absolute bullet drop (inches)

As shown in Table 1 and Table 2, the trajectory at short to medium distances of a 6.5 mm bullet is not significantly affected by the changing air temperature. At 400 meters, only a 3.5 cm difference in bullet drop separates the extreme temperatures. However, when the bullet starts to approach the end of its trajectory, the effect of changing air temperature is greater: the difference between -20 and 30 degrees C (86 to -4 F) is 25 cm (10") at 700 meters. On the other hand, the difference between 20 and 30 degrees C (86-68 F) at 700 meters is only four cm (1.4"), which is marginal and will be difficult to distinguish in practice from other types of errors such as shooting technique. However, if the distance to the target has been measured carelessly, four centimeters can definitely be the difference between hit and miss in a competition setting.

Table 3: 6.5 Creedmoor (Metric)

- 140 gn (9.07 grams) match bullet
- BC (G7): 0.304
- 820 m/s (2690 fps) muzzle velocity
- Relative humidity 40 %
- Air pressure 1015 hPa

Distance (m)

		100	200	300	400	500	600	700
T	30	7.6	31.7	74.4	138	226	342	490
E	20	7.6	31.7	74.7	139	227	344	494
M	10	7.6	31.8	74.9	139.7	229	347	499
P	0	7.6	31.9	75.2	140	230	350	504
(C)	- 10	7.6	32	75.5	141	232	354	510
	- 20	7.6	32.1	75.9	142	234	357	516

Absolute bullet drop (cm)

Table 4: 6.5 Creedmoor (Imperial)

Table 4 is based on the same parameters as table 3 above.

		Distance (yd)						
		100	200	300	400	500	600	700
T	86	2.5	10.4	24.3	44.9	73.3	110	157
E	68	2.5	10.4	24.4	45.1	73.6	110	158
M	50	2.5	10.4	24.4	45.3	74	111	159
P	32	2.5	10.4	24.5	45.5	74.5	112	160
(F)	14	2.5	10.4	24.6	45.7	75	113	162
	-4	2.5	10.5	24.7	46	75.6	114	164

Absolute bullet drop (inches)

The 6.5 Creedmoor shows very similar external ballistic performance to the 6.5x55 mm. It is only when shooting at longer distances, at the end of the trajectory, that there is a significant difference at different temperatures, and only very large differences in temperature will cause a significant change in bullet drop.

Table 5: .308 Winchester (Metric)

- 168 gn (10.89 grams) match bullet
- BC (G7): 0.218
- 808 m/s (2650 fps) muzzle velocity
- Relative humidity 40 %
- Air pressure 1015 hPa

		Distance (m)						
		100	200	300	400	500	600	700
T	30	8	33.8	81	154	258	400	590
E	20	8	33.9	81.4	154	260	404	598
M	10	8	34	81.8	156	262	409	607
P	0	8	34.1	82.3	157	265	415	618
(C)	- 10	8	34.3	82.8	158	268	421	629
	- 20	8	34.4	83.3	160	272	428	642

Absolute bullet drop (cm)

Table 6: .308 Winchester (Imperial)

Table 6 is based on the same parameters as table 5 above.

		\multicolumn{7}{c}{Distance (yd)}						
		100	**200**	**300**	**400**	**500**	**600**	**700**
T	**86**	2.6	11.0	26.3	49.5	82.5	126	185
E	**68**	2.6	11.0	26.4	49.8	83.1	128	187
M	**50**	2.6	11.1	26.5	50.1	83.9	129	190
P	**32**	2.6	11.1	26.7	50.5	84.7	131	193
(F)	**14**	2.6	11.1	26.8	50.9	85.5	132	196
	-4	2.6	11.2	27.0	51.3	86.5	134	199

Absolute bullet drop (inches)

The .308 Winchester generally performs worse in external ballistic terms than the 6.5x55 mm and the 6.5 Creedmoor. This is because the .308 Winchester in our examples has a slower projectile and a significantly lower ballistic coefficient. This is an effect of the original design of the cartridge and is not something we can do much about. The .308 Winchester does not have room in the cartridge for long match bullets, as do the 6.5x55 mm or the Creedmoor, and the longer the bullets we load, the less room there is left for powder in the cartridge. As in the previous example, the differences in bullet trajectories are very marginal at short distances. At 300 meters, the difference between -20 and 30 degrees C (86 to -4 F) is only 2.3 cm (0.9") which is hardly noticeable in any hunting situation. However, the difference is much greater towards the end of the trajectory. At 700 meters, the difference between the extreme temperatures is 52 cm (20"), which can definitely be the difference between a hit and a miss on a target.

The last example is a cartridge better suited to very long-range shooting: the .338 Lapua Magnum. Note that the distances in Table

7 and 8 below are adjusted to better reflect the capabilities of the cartridge.

Table 7: .338 Lapua Magnum (Metric)

- 250 gn (16.2 grams) bullet
- BC (G7): 0.322
- 905 m/s (2970 fps) muzzle velocity
- Relative humidity 40 %
- Air pressure 1015 hPa

Distance (m)

		200	400	600	800	1000	1200	1400
T	30	25.8	111.6	273	532	916	1467	2244
E	20	25.8	112	275	536	927	1490	2288
M	10	25.9	112.5	276	542	939	1516	2340
P	0	25.9	113	278	547	953	1545	2399
(C)	- 10	26	113.6	281	554	969	1579	2467
	- 20	26	114	283	561	986	1616	2542

Absolute bullet drop (cm)

Table 8: .338 Lapua Magnum (Imperial)

Table 8 is based on the same parameters as table 7 above.

Distance (yd)

		200	400	600	800	1000	1200	1400
T	86	8.4	36.3	88.1	169	289	457	688
E	68	8.5	36.4	88.5	171	292	463	700
M	50	8.5	36.5	89.1	172	295	470	714
P	32	8.5	36.7	89.7	174	299	478	729
(F)	14	8.5	36.8	90.3	176	303	487	747
	-4	8.5	37	91	178	308	497	766

Absolute bullet drop (inches)

In the case of the .338 Lapua Magnum, the air temperature becomes a significant problem only at long distances, although it is not insignificant at medium distances. At 600 meters there is a 10 cm (4") difference between the extreme temperatures, which is slightly less than for the 6.5x55 mm, and at 800 meters there is already about 30 cm (11") difference. At the longest distances, the difference between the extreme temperatures amounts to several meters/yards.

Since different calibers are designed to be effective at different distances, the significant impact of the change in air density occurs at different distances for different calibers. A comparison of the four calibers above at 600 meters indicates that the difference in bullet trajectory between the extreme temperatures is ten cm for the .338 Lapua Magnum, 14 cm for the 6.5x55 mm, 15 cm for the 6.5 Creedmoor, and as much as 28 cm for the .308 Winchester. The .308 Winchester is less able to handle changing temperatures than both the 6.5x55 mm and the .338 Lapua Magnum, as a result of both its lower muzzle velocity and its lower ballistic coefficient. This is not something that can be remedied solely by the choice of bullets, powder or rifles, but depends on the performance for which the cartridge was initially designed. The examples above are a good illustration of why some cartridges are better than others for hunting or competitive shooting at longer distances: they can cope with changing atmospheric conditions better than others, and therefore give the shooter or hunter an extra margin of success. A competitive shooter shooting at 700 meters with 6.5x55 has wider margins to make mistakes and still hit the target, than a shooter shooting with .308 Winchester. This is not to say that .308 Winchester is a bad caliber. On the contrary, it is an excellent caliber for most purposes except shooting at very long distances.

Humidity

Air always contains a small amount of water. There is no completely dry air in the atmosphere, but the amount of water vapor in the air can vary. It is somewhat contradictory that relative humidity can be quite high in the winter and lower in the summer. The explanation lies precisely in the concept of *relative humidity*. Cold air cannot contain as much water as warm air, so even if there is a relatively higher humidity in winter, there is less water in *absolute* terms than in the summer.

Wet air is also lighter than dry air. This is counterintuitive because we are used to seeing air as lighter than water. To understand why wet air is lighter than dry air, we need to know Avogadro's law, which states that *a given volume of gas at a certain pressure and temperature always contains the same number of molecules*. No matter what the gas is, it has the same number of molecules within a given volume at the same pressure and temperature. This means that if we add molecules to that volume, other molecules will leave. In this case, when adding the light water molecules consisting of two hydrogen atoms and one oxygen atom, heavier nitrogen and oxygen molecules leave the volume, thus making it lighter. As discussed in a previous chapter, density is defined as mass within a given volume, so when air becomes wet, its density and total mass within a given volume decrease. When a projectile travels through the lower-density wet air, it encounters less resistance than in dry air, and can therefore maintain its velocity better. In this way, there is little difference between changes in air temperature and changes in humidity; both bring about changes in the density of the air, which in turn affects the trajectory of the bullet. There is another way in which humidity can affect the trajectory of the bullet, and that is through liquid water, in the form of rain. We will exemplify these two phenomena in turn.

Impact of humidity

Higher relative humidity results in less bullet drop, and therefore a higher point of impact. The impact of humidity on air density is generally very small in shooting, much smaller than the impact of air temperature, for example. At short to medium distances, it plays virtually no role at all, and is not a variable that needs to be taken into account when shooting at these distances. However, as in the case of air temperature, humidity can have some effect when shooting at very long distances for a given caliber. Such shooting situations include competitive long-range shooting and military sniping, when the aim is to hit a target at the end of the trajectory and with high precision. Humidity is, for hunting, rarely or never a variable that needs to be taken into account.

As mentioned briefly above, the term 'relative humidity' is commonly used rather than absolute humidity. Since warm air has a greater capacity to hold water vapor than cold air, changes in humidity are potentially more of a problem in summer than in winter. This also means that humidity is a more important variable to consider in warm temperatures than in cold ones. It is important to keep in mind that humidity is not a problem just because it is hot outside. Rather, it is a potentially bigger problem when it is hot because changes in humidity cause relatively larger changes in the density of the air. Such a problem would be particularly large if, for example, a competitive shooter from Scandinavia traveled to warmer climates to compete in long-range rifle shooting, but the weapon system and the shooter's ballistic tables are calibrated for the Nordic climate. It would require some adaptation to make the ballistic tables suitable for shooting at warmer temperatures.

Below are some examples that illustrate the relationship between changing humidity and bullet drop. In the tables, only the relative humidity is varied to illustrate how the trajectory changes at different distances. The numbers below each humidity value are the distance that the bullet drops at that distance from the core line, i.e. absolute bullet drop. The relative humidity in northern Europe generally varies between about 40 and 60% when it is not raining, which is why I used those values for the comparison. The highest humidity value, 100% relative humidity, does not necessarily mean that it is raining but there is a lot of moisture in the air, which usually results in fog and dew on the ground.

Impact of humidity on the bullet trajectory

Table 9: 6.5x55 (30° C/86°F)

- 130 gn (8.42 grams) match bullet
- BC (G7): 0.274
- 900 m/s (2950 fps) muzzle velocity
- 30°C (86°F)
- Air pressure 1015 hPa
- RH = relative humidity

Distance in m (≅ yd)	40 % RH	60% RH	100 % RH
300 (330 yd)	62 cm (24")	62 cm (24")	62 cm (24")
600 (660 yd)	289 cm (113")	289 cm (113")	288 cm (113")
900 (980 yd)	771 cm (303")	770 cm (303")	767 cm (302")

Absolute bullet drop

As shown in Table 9 above, the importance of humidity as a single variable is almost insignificant at short and medium distances. Even at long distances for a given caliber, a large difference in humidity doesn't really make a significant difference. The difference at 900 m

($\cong$ 980 yd) for the extreme values of 40% and 100% relative humidity is less than 5 cm or 2 inches, and this is such a small impact that it is hardly meaningful to consider as a separate variable. 900 meters is also quite far for the caliber 6.5x55, and many who shoot at such distances would choose another caliber. But since our intention here is not to assess the suitability of calibers for different distances, but only to analyze the impact of humidity on the bullet path, it is still a relevant example.

The table below illustrates how changing humidity affects the bullet trajectory at a lower temperature. The projectile and parameters of the shot are the same as above, but in this example the temperature is 5° C or 41°F.

Table 10: 6.5x55 (5° C/41° F)

- 130 gn (8.42 grams) match bullet
- BC (G7): 0.274
- 900 m/s (2950 fps) muzzle velocity
- 5° Celsius (41° F)
- Air pressure 1015 hPa

Distance in m ($\cong$ yd)	40 % RH	60% RH	100 % RH
300 (330 yd)	62 cm (24")	62 cm (24")	62 cm (24")
600 (660 yd)	295 cm (116")	295 cm (116")	295 cm (116")
900 (980 yd)	800 cm (315")	800 cm (315")	800 cm (315")

Absolute bullet drop

Table 10 demonstrates how air temperature affects the potential of humidity to change the trajectory of the projectile. When the temperature is 5° C, practically no effect on the trajectory is noted. Even between the extreme values of 40% and 100% relative humidity at 900 meters ($\cong$980 yd), the difference in bullet trajectory drop is less than one cm, which should not play any practical role in precision shooting in competition. The attentive reader will also have noticed the greater difference between Table 9 and Table 10 in terms of absolute bullet drop. This is of course because the temperature in the latter table was lowered by 25 degrees C, which increase the density of the air and thus the resistance that the projectile encounters.

Table 11: .308 Winchester (30°C/86°F)

- 168 gn (10.89 grams) bullet
- BC (G7): 0.218
- 808 m/s (2650 fps) muzzle velocity
- 30°C (86°F)
- Air pressure 1015 hPa
- RH = relative humidity

Distance in m (≅ yd)	40 % RH	60% RH	100 % RH
300 (330 yd)	81 cm (31")	81 cm (31")	81 cm (31")
600 (660 yd)	400 cm (157")	400 cm (157")	398 cm (156")
900 (980 yd)	1166 cm (459")	1162 cm (457")	1155 cm (454")

Absolute bullet drop

As shown in Table 11 above, the impact of changing humidity is practically negligible at common distances for a .308 Winchester. Between the extreme values of 40% and 100% relative humidity at 900 meters, the difference in bullet trajectory drop is 11 cm. In the example, the temperature is 30 degrees C. When the temperature is lower than that, the humidity will have less effect on the bullet trajectory. 900 meters is of course quite a bit outside of the normal range for a .308 Winchester, which also goes to show that humidity in most shooting situations is not a value that needs to be considered. We have to look specifically at the end of trajectories and extreme humidity changes to see significant effects, which are hardly realistic shooting situations. We will look at a final example of a bullet trajectory for the .338 Lapua Magnum.

Table 12: .338 LM (20°C/68°F)

- 250 gn match bullet
- BC (G7): 0.322
- 905 m/s (2970 fps) muzzle velocity
- 20°C (68°F)
- Air pressure 1015 hPa

Distance in m (≅ yd)	40 % RH	60% RH	100 % RH
500 (550 yd)	182 cm (71")	182 cm (71")	182 cm (71")
1000 (1100 yd)	927 cm (365")	926 cm (364")	924 cm (363")
1300 (1420 yd)	1854 cm (730")	1852 cm (729")	1846 cm (726")

Absolute bullet drop

The trajectory for the .338 Lapua Magnum shows a similar pattern to the 6.5x55 and .308 Winchester. As the projectile approaches the end of its trajectory it begins to be significantly more affected by the change in air density. The difference between 40% and 100% relative humidity at 1300 meters is 8 centimeters, which in a competition context could be the difference between hit and miss. At short and medium distances, however, the changing humidity hardly matters.

Water in liquid form - Rain

As has been demonstrated above, higher humidity allows the bullet to travel more easily through the air, as the air as a whole is lighter and is pushed away more easily by the bullet, which therefore impacts the target higher. What about water in liquid form that may be in the air between the shooter and the target? There are some common arguments circulating about this. Some claim that water droplets never hit the bullet, because the pressure wave caused by the bullet evaporates the water before the droplet makes contact with the bullet. Others say that even if the drop hits the bullet, the trajectory is not affected because the drop has such a small mass compared to the kinetic energy of the bullet. But we don't have to speculate; there is knowledge about this based on empirical studies.

The US magazine Guns & Ammo has reported on the issue, using a research facility at the University of *New Mexico Institute of Mining and Technology* to investigate the effect of water droplets on a 125 gn (8.1 gram) .30 caliber bullet.[15] They had access to a high-speed camera with a resolution of 70 000 frames per second which, together with Schlieren technology, provided clear images of the bullet's flight through water droplets. They discovered that the pressure wave from the bullet did not evaporate the water droplet, but that the water came into contact with the bullet. They also discovered, by measuring the angle of the bullet on the film, that the water drop affected the direction of the bullet in a way that could potentially produce a change in impact of as much as 60 cm at 91 meters (100 yards).

These findings are of course very interesting, and show that raindrops can have a significant effect on a bullet if we are unlucky enough to hit a drop. However, it is difficult to say how a bullet is affected in general by contact with a water drop, because a bullet will always hit a drop in different ways. It is also worth noting that they used a very light bullet for .30 caliber, only 125 gn (8.09

---

[15] Guns & Ammo, *Effects of Rain on Bullet Trajectory*, published on 2020-02-06

grams), in the tests. Most competitive .30 caliber shooters use bullets that weigh 168 or 175 grains (10.89 and 11.3 grams, respectively) and would likely be much less affected by colliding with a drop, as there is much more mass in motion. Hunters shooting .308 Winchester can use even heavier bullets up to about 180 gn, and it can be assumed that these would be even less affected. If we take larger calibers such as .338 or .375, it can be assumed that the effect would be even smaller. In any case, it has been proven that water droplets *can* affect the bullet's trajectory, even if they don't always do so, and that this may be something to consider when shooting in wet weather. The fact that water droplets can significantly affect the trajectory of the bullet is probably not so much of interest to sport shooters or hunters as it is to, for example, military snipers, who could potentially miss a target due to the effects of water.

Sunlight, air temperature and wind

The air in the atmosphere does not heat up evenly and predictably. The sun heats the air, but the sun does not shine on all the air at the same time, because sunlight does not reach the whole Earth at the same time. This is a mechanism that creates air masses with different temperatures, densities and pressures that move from one place to another.

The sun not only heats the air directly, but also indirectly by heating the ground. The sun heats the Earth's surface and everything else on it, which in turn heats the air above, but different surfaces absorb different amounts of heat energy from the sun, which means that the air above is heated unevenly. Water, for example, absorbs a lot of thermal energy, while an open field does not absorb as much and therefor heats the air above the ground comparatively more. As the temperature of the air increases, its density and pressure decrease, and it is pushed away by colder and heavier air taking its place. We experience these pressure equalizations between different areas as wind.

Imagine a landscape with some fields, forest, mountains, and a lake. It is a chilly morning, but the sun has just risen and is shining on the landscape. The air layers at the bottom are heated quite differently depending on the surface underneath, and this causes air masses to move between different areas to equalize the air pressure. Over water, the air warms slowly as the water absorbs more thermal energy from the sun. Over mountains and fields, the air layers will heat up faster due to the lower ability of these surfaces to absorb thermal energy. As a result, winds from the water often blow toward land. The air over the lake has a higher density and pressure than that over the fields, and pushes it away.

Understanding these dynamics makes it easier to understand wind as an everyday phenomenon; air is constantly being heated and cooled around us, and due to the varying ability of the ground to absorb heat, the air is heated unevenly. This creates air masses of differing temperature that are almost constantly in motion. When we think about it, it seems strange that there is relatively little wind as often as there is.

GRAVITY AND PROJECTILE TRAJECTORY

Gravity is the external ballistic factor that has the greatest impact on the projectile trajectory after the bullet leaves the barrel. As soon as the projectile leaves the barrel, it is pulled downward in its trajectory due to Earth's gravity. Gravity is a constant and predictable force, and it can be accurately compensated for. To compensate for gravity when shooting, the barrel of a rifle is pointed slightly upwards in relation to the line of sight (LOS), as depicted in Figure 11 below. The line of sight is an imaginary straight line between the rifle sight and the target. When aiming at the target, the sights are pointed straight at the target and the barrel (bore axis) is pointed slightly upwards. The bullet does not fly in a straight line toward the target, but in an arc, first up and then down towards the target. Thus, the line of sight and the bore axis are not parallel to each other.

Figure 11: bullet trajectory

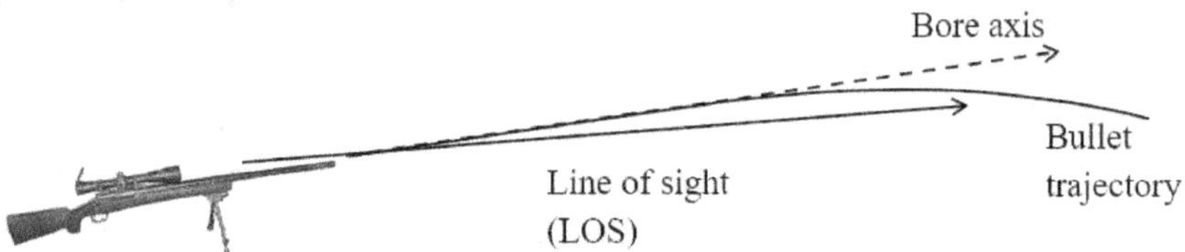

The relationship between the line of sight and the bullet trajectory in the figure above is exaggerated to illustrate the principle. As shown in the figure, the line of sight starts higher than the bullet trajectory. This is also the case in reality, as the rifle scope or iron sights on a rifle are always mounted above the barrel. The bullet typically starts its trajectory below the line of sight, crosses the line of sight in its parabolic trajectory towards the target, and if all goes well impacts the target just where the line of sight meets the target. If the target is very close to the shooter, the bullet may also hit the target below the line of sight on its way upwards in the trajectory. Knowledge of the distances at which the bullet trajectory meets the line of sight can be utilized when sighting in (zeroing) a rifle. In the military for example, some rifles chambered in 7.62 are first sighted in at a distance of 30 meters, and then backed up to 250 meters to verify the adjustment. The trajectory and the line of sight meet at 30 meters, when the projectile is moving upward in its trajectory, and again at 250 meters, when the projectile is moving downward. This way of sighting in a rifle saves time and ammunition.

For a given distance, there are significant variances in the maximum trajectory height between different calibers, projectiles, and velocities. When shooting at medium distances, the maximum trajectory height for common rifle calibers is typically not more than 0.5 meters or yards above the line of sight. At a 1000 meters or yards, the maximum trajectory height is significantly higher: for a .308 Winchester it is more than 5 meters (yards), but for a higher BC cartridge, for example a 6.5, it is closer to 3 meters or yards. When shooting further than 2000 meters, the maximum height of the trajectory can be upward 20-30 meters or yards. A shot at 2500 meters (2730 yds), which is realistic for a caliber like .408 Cheytac, has a maximum bullet trajectory height of 30 meters or 33 yards. The relation between the length of the trajectory and its height is not linear. The longer a ballistic trajectory becomes for a given caliber, the higher the trajectory will be. Below are a number of ballistic tables that illustrate the differences in trajectory height for different cartridges and distances in more detail.

Table 13 below illustrates the maximum trajectory height of different calibers when shooting at 500 meters (appr. 550 yd). The examples in the table represent factory loaded match cartridges with regular jacketed match bullets.

Bullet trajectory height tables

Table 13: bullet trajectory height 500 m

Caliber	6.5x55 mm match 130 gn	.308w match 168 gn	.300 winmag match 190 gn	.338 Lapua Magnum match 250 gn
BC (G7)	.274	.218	.267	.322
Muzzle velocity	900 m/s (2950 fps)	808 m/s (2650 fps)	884 m/s (2900 fps)	905 m/s (2970 fps)
Maximum trajectory height	52 cm (20")	73 cm (29")	54 cm (21")	47 cm (18")
Distance at max height	270 m (295 yd)	280 m (306 yd)	270 m (295 yd)	260 m (284 yd)

As can be noted in table 13, the 338 Lapua Magnum has the lowest trajectory height in the comparison. The .338 Lapua Magnum is a much heavier projectile at 250 gn, and has a significantly higher ballistic coefficient than the other bullets in the comparison. This is primarily due to the fact that the .338 Lapua Magnum was designed as a military sniper cartridge, and it was designed from the outset to shoot long, heavy, high velocity projectiles. As noted in a previous chapter on ballistic coefficients, the relationship between caliber, or diameter, and projectile weight is of great importance to its ballistic coefficient.

In comparison, the .308 Winchester has a significantly higher maximum trajectory height than the 6.5 mm or .338 LM. The .308 Winchester has both a significantly lower ballistic coefficient and lower muzzle velocity than the other calibers in the comparison. I have not selected parameters to make the .308 Winchester look bad. The bullet in the comparison is a good match bullet, at a common weight for the caliber. The differences in ballistic coefficient and velocity are primarily due to two things: one is the weight of the bullet relative to the caliber, and the other is the limited powder capacity of the .308 Winchester. We can load longer and heavier bullets than 168 grain in a .308 Winchester, but when we do that, we can't fit as much powder in the case. Taken together, these things mean that the .308 Winchester is not an optimal choice for long-range shooting.

However, 500 meters is a distance that all of the cartridges in table 13 are designed to handle. The differences between different cartridges become more pronounced when observing examples at longer distances.

Table 14: bullet trajectory height 1000 m

Caliber	6.5x55 mm match 130gn	.308w match 168 gn	.300 winmag match 190 gn	.338 Lapua Magnum match 250 gn
BC (G7)	.274	.218	.267	.322
Muzzle velocity	900 m/s (2950 fps)	808 m/s (2650 fps)	884 m/s (2900fps)	905 m/s (2970 fps)
Maximum trajectory height	3.24 m (3.54 yd)	5.61 m (6.1 yd)	3.49 m (3.81 yd)	3.12 m (3.41 yd)
Distance at max height	560 m (612 yd)	600 m (656 yd)	570 m (623 yd)	550 m (601 yd)

In Table 14, of trajectories at 1000 meters (appr. 1100 yd), it can be noted that the height of the trajectory does not double when the distance is doubled. Instead, the trajectory is about *six times higher*. Thus, the relationship between the length of the trajectory and its height is not linear. In the 308 Winchester, which is the worst cartridge in terms of external ballistics in the comparison, the bullet path is about 7.7 times higher. It is important to understand the relationship between bullet path length and height to understand the potential crosswind effect at the highest point of the bullet path. The longer the distances, the more important this aspect becomes. This is discussed further in the chapter on *wind gradient.*

We will look at another table for bullet trajectories at 1500 meters (1640 yds) to see what a bullet trajectory looks like at those distances for relevant calibers. 6.5x55 mm and .308 Winchester have been removed from the table as they are not suited for shooting at those distances.

Table 15: bullet trajectory height 1500 m

Caliber	.300 winmag match 190 gn	.338 Lapua Magnum match 250 gn
BC (G7)	.267	.322
Muzzle velocity	884 m/s (2900 fps)	905 m/s (2970 fps)
Maximum trajectory height	13.45 m (14.7 yd)	9.6 m (10.49 yd)
Distance at max height	920 m (1000 yd)	875 m (956 yd)

As is evident from table 15, the heavier bullet with the higher ballistic coefficient has a significantly lower maximum trajectory height. The .338 Lapua Magnum has a much lower trajectory than the 300 Winchester Magnum. 1500 meters or yards is certainly at the limit of the capability of the 300 Winchester Magnum, and the caliber was hardly designed for these distances. However, this does not prevent some military forces from using the .300 Winchester Magnum with particularly heavy bullets and high velocity charges for sniping at distances up to 1500 meters.

We will look at a couple more examples of bullet trajectories in the .408 Cheytac caliber, which is a recently developed caliber for precision shooting at very long distances. The bullet in this example is not an ordinary jacketed bullet, but a precision-turned monolithic bullet made from a copper alloy, which allows for an extremely high ballistic coefficient.

Table 16: bullet trajectory height 2000 m

Caliber	.408 Cheytac 419 gn
BC	.949 (G1 mean over 3000 m)
Muzzle velocity	910 m/s (2985 fps)
Maximum height	14.63 m ≅ 16 yd
Distance at maximum height	1140 m (1250 yd)

Table 17: bullet trajectory height 2500 m

Caliber	.408 Cheytac 419 gn
BC	.949 (G1 mean over 3000 m)
Muzzle velocity	910 m/s (2985 fps)
Maximum height	30 m ≅ 33 yd
Distance at maximum height	1480 m (1620 yd)

As tables 16 and 17 above illustrate, bullet trajectories at extremely long distances begin to take on almost absurd forms. A shot at 2500 meters (2730 yds), which is realistic for a caliber like .408 Cheytac, has a maximum trajectory height of 30 meters, and several seconds of flight time to the target. Precision fire with rifles at 2500-3000 meters was almost unthinkable just a few decades ago, but today it is a reality. The .408 Cheytac is also a good example of the high ballistic coefficient of heavy and long bullets. Admittedly, the bullet in the examples above is specified with BC (G1) which gives a higher value than BC (G7), but a ballistic coefficient (G1) close to one is still an absurdly high value for a rifle projectile, and it would have been even higher if the manufacturer had calculated it at a higher velocity instead of using an average value over 3000 meters.

Ballistic coefficient exemplified

The ballistic coefficient has been described above as a measure of a projectile's ability to maintain its velocity in flight. We can use the values in the table above for 1000 meters to make a relative velocity table, and look at how well the different bullets maintain their velocity. We already know the ballistic coefficient of the different bullets, but it can be educational to look at a relative velocity table to see the differences between them expressed as a percentage.

Below is a table of relative velocity loss between different calibers for a 1000-meter shot. The values are the percentage of the muzzle velocity later in the trajectory.

Table 18: relative velocity loss

	.308w	6.5x55 mm	.300 wm	.338LM
500 m	77.5 %	83.3 %	82.5 %	86.2 %
1000 m	55.6 %	67.4 %	65.8 %	72.2 %
1500 m			49.3 %	58 %

One thing that stands out in Table 18 above is how much worse the .308 Winchester maintains velocity compared to the others. However, one should keep in mind that the .308 bullet in the comparison does not actually have bad external ballistic properties; it is just that the other bullets in the comparison have very good external ballistic properties.

Not surprisingly, the .338 Lapua Magnum maintains the velocity the best in the above comparison, as it is a heavy bullet at high velocity with very good ability to overcome air resistance. The 6.5x55 mm with a 130 gn bullet retains its velocity slightly better than the .300 Winchester Magnum with a 190 gn bullet. This is consistent with the BC values since the 6.5x55 mm bullet has a BC (G7) value of .274 and the .30 bullet has a value of .265. This comparison says nothing at all about what impact energy the different projectiles deliver at certain distances, which is a terminal ballistic consideration. If we want to hit something with authority at 1000 meters, the .30 caliber bullet is obviously preferable to the 6.5x55 mm, even though it has a slightly lower ballistic coefficient. However, this need not be the case if the difference in ballistic coefficient had been greater.

Ballistic coefficient and terminal energy

When comparing the terminal energy of two projectiles, where one is lighter but has a higher ballistic coefficient, and the other is heavier but has a lower ballistic coefficient, differences in their terminal energy even out with increasing distance. This is because the heavier bullet with lower BC slows down faster and thus loses its terminal energy faster than the lighter bullet with higher BC, even though the latter started its trajectory with less energy. This is why a .338 Lapua Magnum match bullet has more terminal energy than a standard .50 caliber standard projectile at sufficiently long distances; it is simply a more efficient bullet. In rifle shooting, bigger does not always mean better.

The highest point of the ballistic trajectory

The exact location of the highest point of the trajectory depends on a number of factors, including shooting distance, caliber, muzzle velocity, and ballistic coefficient. When shooting a particular caliber at shorter distances, the target may be hit when the bullet is rising or at its highest point in the trajectory. This is the case, for example, if we shoot a deer at 50 meters with a regular hunting rifle that we sighted in at 100 meters. In this case, the bullet is still rising towards its highest point when it impacts the target.

If we shoot at the distance of 300 meters/yards with a regular hunting caliber, the highest point of the bullet path will be approximately in the middle of the bullet path. As we extend the shooting distance for a particular caliber, the highest point of the bullet moves forward in the trajectory. This is because when shooting at longer distances, the projectile slows down more in the upward phase of the trajectory. When the projectile then turns downward in its trajectory, is has a relatively lower velocity and therefore falls faster to the ground.

We will look at the highest point of the bullet path for some common calibers. The percentage values in the table below indicate the distance at which the bullet reaches its highest point, as a proportion of the total length of the bullet path.

Table 19: the highest point of the trajectory

	.308w	6.5x55 mm	.300 wm	.338LM
500 m (550 yd)	56 % (280 m/306 yd)	54 % (270 m/295 yd)	54 % (270 m/295 yd)	52 % (260 m/284 yd)
1000 m (1100 yd)	60 % (600 m/656 yd)	56 % (560 m/612 yd)	57 % (570 m/623 yd)	55 % (550 m/601 yd)
1500 m (1640 yd)			60 % (900 m/984 yd)	58 % (880 m/962 yd)

As we can see, the highest point at medium distances (500 meters or 550 yds) is just over 50% of the total length of the trajectory. At very long distances for a given caliber, the highest point is instead around 60% of the length of the trajectory, as in the example of the .300 Winchester Magnum at 1500 meters. The longer we shoot with a particular caliber, the further away the highest point of the trajectory moves towards the target. At extremely long distances, the result is that the bullet tends to fall down on the target rather than fly into it.

Flat or curved ballistic trajectory

Sometimes rifle shooters get into discussions about bullet path height and the advantages of a flatter bullet path over a more curved one. Hunters are generally in favor of flatter trajectories, while competitive shooters are not as committed to it even though it may be desirable. This is because hunters have an interest in being able to shoot at a target quickly upon detection, without having to adjust their rifle scope or change the point of aim on the target to hit it. A bullet and load that has a flatter trajectory does not require as much compensation by the shooter to hit near the point of aim at varying distances. A more curved trajectory requires more compensation by the hunter if targets are detected at distances further from the zeroing distance, as the trajectory varies more in elevation.

Apart from the above, there is nothing inherently better about a flatter trajectory. *The goal for every shooter is to hit the target, not to have the flattest trajectory.* The advantage of a flatter trajectory is not to do with the nature of the trajectory, but with the velocity of the projectile; a flatter trajectory means that the projectile has a higher velocity and therefore reaches its target faster than a lower velocity projectile, other variables being equal. The less time a projectile spends in the air, the smaller the bullet drop and wind drift, and the less the shooter has to compensate for these factors. The discussion about flat bullet paths is thus for hunters about being able to shoot faster and more easily at different distances, and for competition shooters mainly about wind rather than the bullet trajectory itself.

There is only one way to flatten the trajectory of a particular cartridge, and that is to fire the projectile at a higher velocity. This can either be done by increasing the velocity of a given projectile, which has its natural limitations in terms of the amount of powder we can fit in a given case volume, or by using a lighter projectile. Both have their advantages and disadvantages. A heavier projectile fired at a higher velocity will cause significantly more recoil and barrel wear. Recoil is for most shooters something that should be minimized, as it affects the accuracy of the shooter. Barrel wear is also something that many shooters want to minimize, as it is a major expense to re-barrel rifles. A rifle designed for long range shooting and shooting heavy projectiles quickly, such as a .300 Winchester Magnum or .338 Lapua Magnum, may need a new barrel after as few as 1000 rounds. This is one of the reasons why many military sniper rifle systems have exchangeable barrels; shooters can practice on the system with a cheaper, slower caliber and then use the heavier, faster caliber more rarely. There are several factors that affect barrel wear, but the primary ones are temperature and pressure which increase when a heavier projectile is fired faster. The advantage of firing a heavier projectile faster is that it drifts less in the wind.

A lighter projectile can be fired at a higher velocity without unmanageable recoil, which is an advantage over a heavier one. A lighter projectile can also provide a flatter trajectory than a heavier projectile, but this comes at the expense of wind sensitivity.

Muzzle velocity and vertical dispersion

Vertical dispersion is a measure of how much the bullet strikes spread vertically around the point of aim on a target. The vertical dispersion of projectiles can also be affected by wind, as discussed in the later chapter on wind drift. A consistent muzzle velocity is always desirable, in hunting as well as in competition shooting, although it becomes increasingly more important with increased shooting distance. The smaller the target and the longer the distance, the more important is a consistent muzzle velocity in order to hit the target.

For instance, when shooting a 6.5 Creedmoor at 800 meters ($\cong$ 870 yd) the vertical spread will be about 40 cm or 15 inches when muzzle velocity varies 20 m/s or 65 fps. This is significant vertical dispersion that might well cause a miss in competition. A muzzle velocity variance of 20 m/s is unfortunately not uncommon in factory-loaded ammunition. I have measured bigger variances in factory-loaded ammunition labeled as "match" ammunition.

Vertical dispersion tables

Table 20: 6.5x55 mm - 500 m

- 130 gn (8.42 grams) match bullet
- BC (G7): 0.274
- 900 m/s (2950 fps) muzzle velocity
- 15°C (59° F)
- Air pressure 1015 hPa

Muzzle velocity	Point of impact at 500 meters ($\cong$ 550 yd)
V_0 = 900 m/s (2950 fps)	(center hit)
V_0 = 890 m/s (2919 fps)	-4.2 cm (-1.6")
V_0 = 880 m/s (2887 fps)	-10 cm (-3.9")

Table 21: 6.5x55 - 800 m

Table 21 is based on the same parameters as for the projectile in Table 20 above.

Muzzle velocity	Point of impact at 800 meters ($\cong$ 870 yd)
V_0 = 900 m/s (2950 fps)	(center hit)
V_0 = 890 m/s (2919 fps)	-15 cm (-5.9")
V_0 = 880 m/s (2887 fps)	-30 cm (-11.8")

At 500 meters, a 20 m/s (65 fps) change in muzzle velocity causes 10 cm (3.9") of vertical dispersion. At 800 meters/870 yd, a vertical dispersion of 30 cm (11.8") is caused when the variation in muzzle velocity is 20 m/s. A 20 m/s muzzle velocity extreme spread is more variation than we should have in competition ammunition. 800 meters is a fairly long shot for the 6.5x55 mm, but it does occur in competition.

Table 22: 6.5 Creedmoor – 800 m

- 140 gn (9.07 grams) match bullet
- BC (G7): 0.304
- 820 m/s (2690 fps) muzzle velocity
- Relative humidity 40 %.
- Air pressure 1015 hPa

Muzzle velocity	Point of impact at 800 meters ($\cong$ 870 yd)
V_0 = 820 m/s (2690 fps)	(center hit)
V_0 = 810 m/s (2657 fps)	-20 cm (-7.8")
V_0 = 800 m/s (2624 fps)	-40 cm (-15.8")

The projectiles of the caliber 6.5 Creedmoor are similar to those of the 6.5x55 mm in their external ballistic performance. The vertical dispersion, at a difference in muzzle velocity of just or 20 m/s or 65 fps, is significant.

Table 23: .300 Winchester Magnum - 1200 m

- 190 gn (12.31 grams) match bullet
- BC (G7): 0.267
- 884 m/s (2900 fps) muzzle velocity
- 15° C (59° F)
- Air pressure 1015 hPa

Muzzle velocity	Point of impact at 1200 meters ($\cong$ 1310 yd)
V_0 = 884 m/s (2900 fps)	(center hit)
V_0 = 874 m/s (2867 fps)	-52 cm (-20")
V_0 = 864 m/s (2834 fps)	-107 cm (-42")

Table 24: .338 Lapua Magnum - 1200 m

- 250 gn (16.2 grams) match bullet
- BC (G7): 0.322
- 905 m/s (2970 fps) muzzle velocity
- 15° C (59° F)
- Air pressure 1015 hPa

Muzzle velocity	Point of impact at 1200 meters ($\cong$ 1310 yd)
V_0 = 905 m/s (2970 fps)	(center hit)
V_0 = 895 m/s (2936 fps)	-40 cm (-15.8")
V_0 = 885 m/s (2903 fps)	-81 cm (-31")

As can be seen from Tables 23 and 24, the .338 Lapua Magnum handles variation in muzzle velocity better than the .300 Winchester Magnum at 1200 meters. The .338 Lapua Magnum in the example has only 21 m/s or 68 fps higher muzzle velocity than the .300

Winchester Magnum, but a significantly heavier bullet and higher BC, which makes all the difference. As is evident from Tables 23 and 24, a significant spread in muzzle velocity makes a big change in the point of impact at 1200 meters with these two calibers.

WIND DRIFT

Wind drift is not the biggest external ballistic influence on shooting, but wind drift is often the biggest challenge. Wind drift is a variable that cannot be compensated for as easily as many other variables discussed in this book. Wind is sometimes referred to as a *non-deterministic variable*, which means that it is impossible to know exactly how the wind will affect a projectile in flight. Gravity, on the other hand, is constant at a certain distance from the Earth's surface. Gravity is a deterministic variable, because we can predict exactly what effect it will have on a projectile in a given situation. The same goes for the Coriolis effect. Its causes are complex, but its effect is deterministic and we have mathematical formulae to calculate it. In theory, wind can be fully compensated for, but this requires knowing exactly what the wind pattern is between the shooter and the target, as well as how the wind pattern will change during the bullet's flight. It also assumes that all the variables involved can be collected, calculated and compensated for before the wind has changed enough to render the final ballistic solution obsolete. We call the wind drift non-deterministic because it is practically impossible to solve the above task for a single shooter during hunting or shooting. The possibility that remains for us is to use sensors, anemometers, eyes, ears and touch as well as tables, feeling and experience to come up with a ballistic solution that is good enough for the particular shooting situation.

All the above is the reason why wind reading and wind compensation is a somewhat mysterious skill in shooting. Skill in reading wind patterns always comes from long and elusive experience, but the result of that experience appears to an outside observer as an almost supernatural ability. By the term "wind reading" I don't just mean sensing the speed of the wind, which is the easy part, but rather reading the wind's flow through a certain terrain, understanding where the wind will affect the bullet the most in a given situation, and quickly translating that understanding into practical action that will results in hitting the target. A positive aspect of wind and wind reading is that these skills can be practiced virtually anywhere, by observing the effect of different winds on different types of vegetation.

Wind drift is often in practice greater than most shooters think. This is partly because most shooters *tend to underestimate wind strength,* and partly because they don't understand that the *crosswind effect is greater than we think* when we are not familiar with the physics and math around it.

Wind drift is linear with respect to variations in wind speed. Assuming that a constant two-second crosswind causes a drift of 4 cm at a certain distance, a 100% increase in wind speed will also cause a 100% increase in drift, meaning that the wind drift will be 8 cm. This relationship is linear. However, the wind drift is not the same *over the entire* trajectory of the projectile given a constant crosswind. This is due to the varying velocity of the projectile. We will discuss these aspects in more detail in the sections below, but first we will discuss why wind drift occurs at all.

The mechanism of wind drift

The intuitive view of how wind drift occurs is that the wind blows the projectile from its path. This is not technically correct, but it is a very strong and intuitive view of what happens when the bullet drifts sideways. We see objects blowing around every day: candy wrappers, plastic bags, flags and more. It's easy to imagine that it works the same way with the bullets we shoot. But the objects we see blowing around every day are *neither gyroscopically stabilized projectiles, nor do they travel at supersonic velocities,* so the intuitive understanding of the mechanism of wind drift is incorrect.

What happens to a gyroscopically stabilized projectile is that it tends to be angled into the crosswind. If the wind is blowing from the left in the direction of fire, the bullet responds by turning (yawing) very slightly into the wind flow, and away from the straight horizontal line towards the target. The reason the bullet turns into the wind is that the drag increases on the side of the bullet that the wind is blowing towards. The velocity of the bullet on the windward side is slowed down due to the increased drag, and the result is that the bullet tends to yaw into the wind flow. The bullet's gyroscopic stabilization prevents it from turning too much into the wind flow, and the yaw angle into the wind flow is usually stated as less than one degree, but this small angle is enough to cause wind drift. The bullet then flies with the tip slightly to the side on its trajectory towards the target while air resistance slows the bullet down. But the air resistance acting along the axis of rotation of the bullet is no longer directed straight backwards, along a straight line between the shooter and the target, but diagonally across that line and towards the opposite side. It is this force that causes the projectile to veer off the intended trajectory. Figure 12 below is a bullet seen from above in its flight towards the target. In Figure 12, the angle of the bullet in relation to the trajectory towards the target (red arrow) is exaggerated.

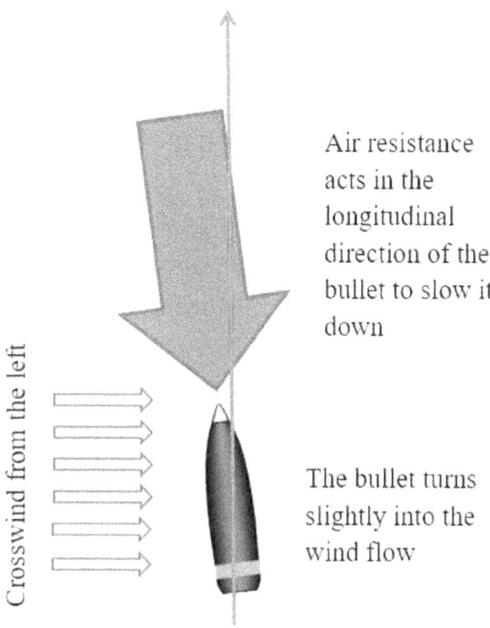

The bullet turns very slightly into the wind flow due to the increased drag on the left side, while the general air resistance acts on the longitudinal axis of the bullet to slow it down. This force is not directed straight backwards along the sight line, but is directed slightly diagonally across it and to the right. This means that the bullet, as it travels on its path towards the target, is not only slowed down by drag but also drifts to the right away from its original path. *The stronger the crosswind, the more the projectile is directed into the airflow and the greater the resulting wind drift.*

When we understand the actual cause of wind drift, which is the air resistance acting along the length of the bullet, it is clear why a bullet with a higher ballistic coefficient drifts less in a given crosswind than a bullet with a lower BC. The bullet with a higher ballistic coefficient experiences less air resistance overall, the drag force acting diagonally across the line of sight is weaker and thus the resulting wind drift is also less.

Impact of wind on the projectile trajectory

Crosswinds are a potentially very powerful influence on the ballistic trajectory, and it is usually not an option to completely ignore them. Exceptions are hunting shots at shorter distances below 100 meters or yards. In this case, it takes a very strong crosswind to significantly affect the bullet trajectory of a common hunting caliber such as .308, 30-06 or .270 Winchester. However, for hunting at longer distances, and for all forms of precision competition shooting, crosswinds are always a variable to consider.

Below is a set of tables for different calibers that exemplify the lateral wind drift at different distances and wind speeds. In the examples, we assume that the wind blows perpendicular to the bullet path (full value wind). This is rarely the case in reality, but we will discuss later how to calculate the real crosswind effect. The gyroscopic drift is excluded from the examples below, and thus they only show the wind drift. In reality, rifle bullets will drift more to the right in a given crosswind from the left due to the fact that the gyroscopic drift also causes the projectile to drift to the right, given that the rifling in the given barrel rotates clockwise. When the wind blows from the right, on the other hand, the projectile will drift less to the left because the gyroscopic drift to the right compensates to some extent for the wind drift. This effect on the trajectory is something to consider at longer ranges, although typically, modern ballistic calculators automatically change the required adjustments for wind drift to accommodate gyroscopic drift, so that the shooter doesn't have to.

In the examples below, it is also assumed that the wind speed is constant during the trajectory all the way to the target. This is rarely the case in reality, except at shorter distances. Wind speed can vary a lot over a surface, and especially over longer distances. However, as the examples below are intended to provide an overall understanding of the effect of wind on the trajectory, we will allow the tables to not perfectly represent an actual trajectory. The ballistic tables exemplifying the effect of wind drift on the projectile trajectory are presented both in a metric and in an imperial version, as they would have appeared too cluttered and unclear with both metric and imperial included into one.

Impact of wind on the projectile trajectory

Table 25: 6.5x55 mm (Metric)

- 130 gn (8.42 grams) match bullet
- BC (G7): 0.274
- 900 m/s (2950 fps) muzzle velocity
- 15° C (59° F)
- Air pressure 1015 hPa
- Relative humidity 40 %
- Wind direction 90 degrees from the bullet trajectory

WINDSPEED

	Distance (m)						
	100	200	300	400	500	600	700
2 m/s	1	3	7	13	21	32	46
4 m/s	1.5	6	14	27	43	65	91
6 m/s	2	9	22	40	65	97	137
8 m/s	3	12	29	53	86	129	183
10 m/s	4	16	36	67	108	162	229
12 m/s	5	19	44	80	130	194	275

Wind drift (cm)

Table 26: 6.5x55 mm (Imperial)

Table 26 is based on the same parameters as Table 25 above.

W		Distance (yd)						
I		100	200	300	400	500	600	700
N	4 mph	0.2	0.9	2.1	4	6	9	13
D	8 mph	0.4	1.8	4.3	7	12	18	26
S	12 mph	0.7	2.7	6.4	11	18	28	39
P	16 mph	0.9	3.7	8.5	15	25	37	53
E	20 mph	1.1	4.6	10.6	19	31	46	66
E	24 mph	1.3	5.5	13	23	38	56	79
D		Wind drift (inches)						

Table 27: 6.5 Creedmoor (Metric)

- 140 gn (9.07 grams) match bullet
- BC (G7): 0.304
- 820 m/s (2690 fps) muzzle velocity
- 15° C (59° F)
- Relative humidity 40 %
- Air pressure 1015 hPa
- Wind direction 90 degrees from the bullet trajectory

W		Distance (m)						
I		100	200	300	400	500	600	700
N	2 m/s	0.8	3	7	13	21	32	35
D	4 m/s	1.5	6	14	27	43	65	92
S	6 m/s	2.3	9	22	40	65	98	138
P	8 m/s	3.1	12	29	54	87	130	183
E	10 m/s	3.8	15	36	67	109	163	229
E	12 m/s	4.6	19	44	81	131	195	275
D		Wind drift (cm)						

Table 28: 6.5 Creedmoor (Imperial)

Table 28 is based on the same parameters as Table 27 above.

W				Distance (yd)				
I		100	200	300	400	500	600	700
N	4 mph	0.2	0.9	2.2	4.0	6	9	13
D	8 mph	0.5	1.9	4.4	8	13	19	27
S	12 mph	0.7	2.8	6.6	12	19	29	40
P	16 mph	0.9	3.8	8.8	16	26	38	43
E	20 mph	1.2	4.7	11	20	32	48	67
E	24 mph	1.4	5.6	13	24	38	57	80
D					Wind drift (inches)			

Table 29: .308 Winchester (Metric)

- 168 gn (10.89 grams) match bullet
- BC (G7): 0.218
- 808 m/s (2650 fps) muzzle velocity
- 15° C (59° F)
- Air pressure 1015 hPa
- Relative humidity 40 %
- Wind direction 90 degrees from the bullet trajectory

W				Distance (m)				
I		100	200	300	400	500	600	700
N	2 m/s	1	5	11	21	34	52	75
D	4 m/s	2	9	22	41	68	103	149
S	6 m/s	3	14	33	62	102	155	224
P	8 m/s	4	19	44	82	136	207	298
E	10 m/s	6	23	55	103	170	258	373
E	12 m/s	7	28	66	124	204	310	448
D					Wind drift (cm)			

Table 30: .308 Winchester (Imperial)

Table 30 is based on the same parameters as Table 29 above.

WINDSPEED	Distance (yd)	100	200	300	400	500	600	700
	4 mph	0.3	1.4	3	6	9	15	21
	8 mph	0.7	2.7	6	12	19	29	42
	12 mph	1	4	9	18	29	44	63
	16 mph	1.3	5.5	13	24	39	59	85
	20 mph	1.7	6.9	16	30	49	74	106
	24 mph	2	8.2	19	36	59	88	127

Wind drift (inches)

Table 31: .300 Winchester Magnum (Metric)

- 190 gn (12.31 grams) match bullet
- BC (G7): 0.267
- 884 m/s (2900 fps) muzzle velocity
- 15° C (59° F)
- Air pressure 1015 hPa
- Relative humidity 40 %.
- Wind direction 90 degrees from the bullet trajectory

WINDSPEED	Distance (m)	100	300	500	700	900	1100	1300
	2 m/s	0.8	8	24	52	95	159	244
	4 m/s	1.7	16	49	105	191	318	488
	6 m/s	2.5	24	73	157	286	478	732
	8 m/s	3.3	32	98	210	382	637	976
	10 m/s	4.2	40	122	262	478	796	1220
	12 m/s	5	48	147	315	573	956	1464

Wind drift (cm)

Table 32: .300 Winchester Magnum (Imperial)

Table 32 is based on the same parameters as Table 31 above.

		100	300	500	700	900	1100	1300
W				Distance (yd)				
I	4 mph	0.2	2.4	7	15	27	44	68
N	8 mph	0.4	4.8	14	30	54	89	137
D	12 mph	0.7	7.2	21	45	81	133	206
S	16 mph	1	9.6	28	60	108	178	275
P	20 mph	1.2	11.9	35	75	135	222	343
E	24 mph	1.5	14.3	42	90	162	267	412
E				Wind drift (inches)				
D								

The tables above are also an illustration of how important ballistic coefficient is in regards to wind drift. If we compare 6.5x55 mm and .308 Winchester, we see that 6.5x55 mm at 600 meters or 650 yards in 10 m/s has a 38% less drift, 162 cm (64 inches) compared to .308 Winchester's 258 cm (101 inches).

Crosswind near or far away

A common question is which crosswind is most important: near the shooter, in the middle of the trajectory or near the target? Sometimes we hear shooters arguing about it, and they're actually all correct. All crosswind matters, but exactly which wind is most important at the moment depends very much on the specific shooting situation.

- Crosswind closer to the shooter is important because the lateral acceleration it imparts to the bullet remains all the way to the target, provided that crosswind from the other direction does not affect the bullet as much in the opposite direction.

- Crosswind closer to the target has a greater relative effect on the bullet than it did earlier in the trajectory, because the bullet travels more slowly and the wind therefore affects the bullet for a longer time over a given distance, resulting in greater drift.

- In the middle of the trajectory, the wind may have a greater impact because wind speed increases with altitude. The increase with height is called the *wind gradient* or *wind speed gradient*. The effect of the wind gradient on the wind drift of a rifle bullet is highly dependent on the length of the trajectory. Shots at short and medium distances have, depending on the caliber, a bullet trajectory height no higher than about one meter or approximately one yard, and the wind gradient is therefore negligible in most cases. It is only at long ranges, or when shooting in mountainous terrain or similar conditions that wind gradient can be important. Extremely long shots (>2500 m) can have a bullet trajectory height of 30 meters (90 ft) or more, so in these cases the wind gradient is much more significant. For lightweight bullets, such as .22lr, wind gradient can be important, for example when shooting from a height or downward slope towards a target. The wind tends to be stronger off the edge of the slope, so the bullet may change direction unexpectedly. Shooting off of slopes or mountain sides can be very tricky.

In theory, however, the wind at the beginning of the trajectory is most important, because the sideways acceleration created by the crosswind continues all the way to the target. This does not mean, however, that crosswind at the beginning of the trajectory is always the most important. As we have seen above, crosswind in the middle and the end of a trajectory can also play important roles, and the definitive importance of crosswinds at different stages of the trajectory will differ from one shooting situation to another.

The limitations of ballistic calculators

Ballistic calculators are great tools for hitting targets, and are particularly important for long-range shooting. However, they have clear limitations regarding wind. Ballistic calculators generally treat wind as a deterministic variable, even though it is not. We input a wind speed and the direction the wind is coming from, and the calculator provides a ready-made solution for how much impact the wind has on the specific shot. The solution provided by the calculator assumes that the effect of the wind on the projectile is constant throughout the trajectory. But in reality, the wind rarely has a constant effect on a projectile over its entire flight path, and at very long distances it almost never does. We can certainly get very far by observing and correctly compensating for base winds, but this solution is never perfect. We return to base wind and practical strategies for dealing with wind later in the book.

However, ballistic calculators cannot be blamed for shortcomings in wind compensation. First of all, it is very difficult in practice to collect accurate values for wind speeds and their directions over the length and height of a given trajectory Secondly, it would be practically almost impossible to try to input these values and get a ready-made ballistic solution in a reasonable time to shoot before the wind has changed again. The conclusion is that ballistic calculators are excellent tools for deterministic variables such as gravity, gyroscopic drift, Coriolis effect etc., but for wind they have their limitations.

Crosswind

A phenomenon that causes particular headache in shooting, and especially shooting at long distances, is crosswind. By crosswind I mean not only single crosswinds, but also conflicting crosswinds, blowing in the opposite direction from each other but at different distances. This is actually not an uncommon phenomenon, but the risk of conflicting crosswinds obviously increases the longer the distances are. It is unusual for winds to blow against each other over a distance of 100 meters, but not that unusual at 1000 meters. We can see this on longer ranges that have wind pennants set up along the range. A pennant at 100 meters may be straight to the right and one at 800 meters straight to the left. This is another example of how wind reading and wind compensation is a skill that cannot be based solely on the ability to use ballistic calculators. Rather, it is a matter of observation, wind speed estimation and experience that together provide a sense of how the crosswinds will affect the projectile. Ultimately, it is the shooter's knowledge, experience and intuition that determines whether to turn the wind turret five or seven clicks to the right or left, and depending on different variables such as distance, caliber and target, it can be the difference between a hit and a miss. When it comes to managing wind drift, there is no substitute for practice.

Crosswind effect

Crosswind is not the same as *crosswind effect*. Crosswind effect is very central to understanding the effect that wind has on a projectile. Crosswind effect is also an often-misunderstood concept, and one can find many incorrect descriptions of crosswind and crosswind effect on the web. Crosswind is the strength of the wind expressed in a measure such as meters per second or miles per hour. Crosswind effect, on the other hand, is the *effect that the crosswind has on the projectile, depending on the angle from which the wind is blowing in relation to the trajectory.* Crosswind and crosswind effect are almost never identical, although they can be very similar. Figure 13 below illustrates how the crosswind effect changes with the angle of the wind to the trajectory. The large arrow represents the direction of the shot, and the numbers along the right edge of the protractor represent the crosswind effect as percentage of a full-value wind, i.e., 90 degrees from the trajectory, at different angles to the trajectory.

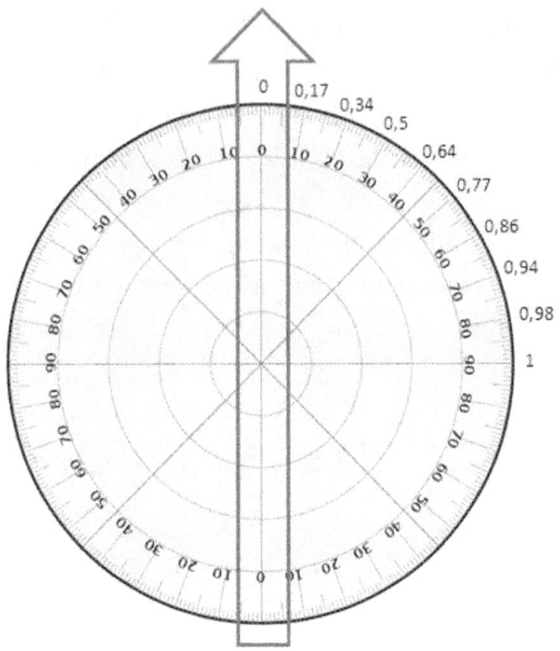

To explain the crosswind effect, let's consider a practical example and use Figure 13 above to find the answer. Let's say that we are going to shoot at 500 meters, and that there is a 5 m/s (11 mph) full-value crosswind from the right. In this case, we need to compensate for a 5 m/s (11 mph) wind speed, because the crosswind and the crosswind effect are the same when the wind blows perpendicular to the path of the bullet. In the figure above, we see that a full-value wind, a wind that is perpendicular to the path of the bullet, has a value of one and the crosswind effect is therefore 100% of the crosswind.

Let's say instead that the 5 m/s (11 mph) crosswind does not blow perpendicular to our bullet trajectory, but instead 45 degrees from it, i.e., from 1:30 if we think of the clock as a comparison. This is known as a half-value wind. What crosswind effect does the wind have in that case? Many people naturally answer 2.5 m/s (5.5 mph) on that question, since it is half of 5 m/s and 45 degrees is half of 90 degrees. But this is wrong. The correct answer, as shown in the table above, is that the crosswind effect is:

$$5 \times 0.7 = 3.5 \text{ m/s } (11 \times 0.7 = 7.7 \text{ mph})$$

If we had fired the shot at 500 meters, and adjusted for a 2.5 m/s (5.5 mph) crosswind instead of 3.5 (7.7) as it actually is, we would probably have missed the target or injured the game, depending on what the target is and what caliber we use. However, if we had misjudged the angle of the wind to the trajectory, and it was 55 degrees instead of 45, the crosswind effect would have been:

$$5 \times 0.82 = 4.1 \text{ m/s}$$

This would of course also have created difficulties for the shot in question, albeit not as big.

The differences between the crosswind effect and the wind speed are due to the fact that the *crosswind effect does not change linearly with the angle of the wind; instead, it changes with the sine of the angle*. The sine is a trigonometric function, i.e., a certain measure of a triangle. The sine of an angle is calculated by dividing the length of the opposite side by the length of the hypotenuse. Figure 13 above contains all the information we need to calculate the crosswind effect in practice, and we do not need to be more precise than that in our calculations. We should also bear in mind that it can be difficult to determine exactly what angle the wind is blowing from in relation to the bullet trajectory. In many practical shooting situations, and hunting in particular, it is usually not necessary to assess the direction of the wind with an accuracy of 10 degrees. At short ranges, 15-20 degrees should be sufficient for most purposes. But as usual, the rule is that the more accurate the measurement the more accurate the results.

There are a few things I want to emphasize about crosswind effect. As shown in figure 13 above, one third of the crosswind effect of a full-value wind is present already at an angle of 20 degrees, and half of the crosswind effect of a full-value wind is present at an angle of 30 degrees. At a crosswind angle of 45 degrees to the trajectory, the crosswind effect is already 70 % of a full-value wind. This means that most people tend to underestimate the crosswind effect. Our intuitive understanding of the crosswind effect is usually wrong, and we need mathematics and tables to correct that understanding.

The second important thing to note from Figure 13 above is that all angles above 70 degrees from the bullet trajectory can, for most rifle shooting purposes, be counted as a full wind value. This is because already at 60 degrees the crosswind effect is 86% of a full-value crosswind, and at 70 degrees it is about 90%. An exception to this rule would be a long-range precision match, where a very precise ballistic solution is required to hit the target.

However, the fact that we have a poor intuitive understanding of crosswind effect does not mean that we should always turn the turrets on the rifle scope more to compensate for crosswind. When shooting at long distances, the crosswind effect is rarely constant all the way to the target. This means that if we compensate for a given crosswind effect, based on a crosswind that we have measured correctly, we will probably overcompensate for the wind. My own experience from competition tells me that it is better to carefully turn the wind turret when compensating for crosswind. If my wind table for a 600-meter shot with a 6.5x55 mm says I should compensate eight clicks (0.8 MRAD) for a 4 m/s (9 mph) crosswind effect, I would rather start with six clicks and try to see in the rifle scope whether I hit or missed the target on the first shot. When competing with rifle scopes, we often have the luxury of being able to see the bullet holes on the target through the scope, which greatly facilitates wind compensation. Aperture sight shooters don't have that advantage, and have to rely on knowledge and experience to shoot the whole series of shots and hope they get it right. At the end of this book, I have included a tool for determining crosswind effect that I myself use when shooting. I hope that it can be useful for you as well.

Base wind

As a shooter or hunter, it can be beneficial to gain an understanding of the larger patterns of wind movement, i.e., its cycles. Such wind cycles last for different lengths of time, and depend on different mechanisms depending on the scale of the wind movement. At the global level, the giant wind movements are primarily due to (1) warmer air rising at the Equator and moving north and south towards the poles and (2) the circular movement of the wind in the northern and southern hemispheres caused by the Coriolis effect. The Coriolis effect is discussed in detail in a later chapter. The large global wind patterns can affect the weather and wind over several countries at the same time. At a regional scale, wind movements are primarily dictated by the greater ability of the sea to absorb thermal energy than land. The air density over water is higher than over land, and cool air tends to blow towards the coast from the sea. At the local level, in addition to the larger effects above, wind flows are dictated by how the air is heated and cooled, as well as how the surrounding terrain affects the ability of the air to move between areas of high and low pressure. These local flows during the day usually last several hours and change with the rising or setting of the sun. This kind of local wind can be called a *base wind,* because it lasts for a longer period of time, often a few hours, and often moves in roughly the same direction. When shooting competitively or hunting, it's good to have an idea of what the base wind is like at our location so we can compensate for it more quickly before shooting. For hunting, it's even more important because many species of game have senses of smell that are many times more sensitive than ours. They can smell a hunter from hundreds or even thousands of meters away, so we have to approach the game upwind. Below, base wind and practical wind management strategies are discussed in more detail.

Perfection or practicality

One trap we fall into when shooting competitively is seeking perfection when it is not necessary. This is something that often unites long-range shooters. We tend to be very particular about riles, rifle scopes, ammunition and ballistic tables, and tend to always look for that perfect shot. This is of course a must for military snipers, as they often have to hit the target in the right place with their first shot. However, it is not always a requirement for competition shooters. It can therefore be a good idea to have an idea of how much margin of error we have in different wind speeds at different distances, while still hitting the target. I bring up this topic before we discuss strategies for dealing with wind drift, because otherwise it is easy to fall into the trap of trying to do everything perfectly all the time. Sometimes it may be tactically smarter to complete the task faster and move on to the next shot.

Since long-range shooters usually have bullets with high ballistic coefficients and high muzzle velocities, it is often not even necessary to adjust for wind at medium distances, depending on the target and accuracy requirements. We may instead be able to hold the reticle on one side of the target to hit the bullseye; this method is called "hold-off", or more colloquially "Kentucky windage". Or, if we are under time pressure and we are not scoring points on the specific target but only hits, such as when shooting at steel targets at long distances, it may be worth shooting faster and getting a hit on one side of the target instead of in the middle. These are often practically intelligent strategies for getting quick hits, which may be overlooked because we are looking for a perfect result when it is not a must. We can ask ourselves before shooting: what kind of precision do I need to achieve my goals with this shoot? Do I need to hit every single target in the center or should I prioritize speed? This also has to do with whether the shooting itself is performed under time pressure or not. There is nothing wrong with pursuing perfection if we have all the time in the world to do so. However, during competitions we often have to compromise between measuring distance and wind speed, making adjustments and shooting technique. With limited time, it is often not possible to do everything to perfection and we have to prioritize tasks. It is a good idea to understand how much drift a particular crosswind causes at different distances, in order to understand when it is not that important to make precise adjustments, and when it is absolutely necessary to do so. This knowledge can only be reached by studying ballistic tables, as well as testing the predicted trajectories on the range.

Consider Table 25, in an earlier chapter, for 6.5x55 mm. Suppose we are to fire a shot at 400 meters ($\cong$ 440 yd) in a 6 m/s (13 mph) crosswind at a paper or steel target. If we have a good knowledge of the drift of a specific charge and projectile, and if we know the approximate size of the target, it is much faster to just hold off 40 cm to compensate for the wind instead of making adjustments to the rifle scope. In addition, anyone shooting with a rifle scope intended for competition shooting probably has reticle that corresponds to one or another angular measurement, milliradians (MRAD) or minutes of angle (MOA), which can be used to hold off from the target.[16]

Dealing with crosswind

When hunting at very short distances, a very strong full-value wind is required to cause significant wind drift. However, at slightly longer hunting distances of around 200 meters with a regular hunting rifle, such as a .308 Winchester or a 30-06 Springfield, a crosswind of 5-7 m/s (11-15 mph) can be enough to cause the bullet to miss the vital zone of a larger animal. Therefore, the hunter should know his bullet trajectory and be able to compensate for this. The examples above are, of course, generalizations based on what calibers are commonly used for hunting, and what muzzle velocities common hunting projectiles usually have. Hunting bullets that have a high ballistic coefficient and travel at high velocity will be less affected by wind. In practice, wind drift in short range hunting situations is a relatively minor problem, and the rest of this chapter will deal with wind drift for long-range precision shooting.

---

[16] Later chapters in this book include a discussion of different angular measurements and conversions between them.

As we have already discussed, crosswind is the second largest factor affecting the bullet path, or actually the potentially second largest factor since there is sometimes no wind. But since gravity is easy to compensate for, given that we know an approximate distance to the target, the crosswind in practical shooting often appears to be the biggest problem. When we know how far we are going to shoot, we just look at our table and turn the elevation turret on the scope to hit the target at the correct height. On the other hand, when shooting at longer distances, the crosswind must be estimated, the angle determined, and then compensated for, which in practice is almost always more work than compensating for gravity. Of course, we may *sometimes* need to compensate for the angle of the trajectory as well, when shooting up or down, which is dealt with in a later chapter, but for the wind we always have to consider the angle.

It is useful for anyone who shoots at long distances to have detailed data on how crosswinds at different speeds affect the projectiles they fire from a certain rifle. The more careful we are in our preparations, and the more we practice with our rifle, the easier it will be to compensate for crosswinds. It is a good idea to have a detailed table of how our projectiles are affected by different crosswind speeds at different distances. We can call this a *Main wind table*. This kind of table can in turn be used in different methods for dealing with wind.

Low-high

Low-high is a handy strategy for use in competition or hunting. It involves measuring (or assessing) the wind speed at the competition or hunting ground *before* the start of the activity. We measure the wind speed in an area for a few minutes, noting the lowest stable wind speed as well as the highest stable wind speed. We can also note the highest values in the form of gusts, should we be forced to shoot in a gust later, which should of course be avoided if possible. Once we have done this, we have our *low base wind* and our *high base wind*. It can also be a good idea to note how the local vegetation behaves during the low and high base winds. This is because we cannot always stand up with an anemometer while shooting or hunting, and we may have to assess the approximate wind strength based on the vegetation from the shooting site where we are located. If we are shooting in the prone position, it is a good idea to lie down while measuring the wind speed to feel how that wind speed feels against our skin in the current temperature and humidity. The wind speed increases with height, and is always significantly lower closer to the ground, so it can be good to familiarize ourselves with how the wind feels lower down at a certain wind speed when shooting in the prone position. Note that it can be difficult to learn general rules about how different plant species move at different wind speeds, because the same species can have different characteristics depending on where it grows. For example, trees and shrubs on mountains tend to grow lower and stiffer than the same species at a lower altitude. They are therefore steadier in the wind, and will not show the same sensitivity to wind as in a lower altitude. Therefore, if we are traveling a long distance to participate in a shooting event, it is a good idea to observe the plants and trees at the location where we are going to shoot.

When we have measured our low and high base winds, we go back to our main wind table to see what adjustments we need to make to compensate for the crosswind in different increments between these wind speeds. We can then write these adjustments down on a notepad that we have easily accessible, or even better on a writing card that we can attach to our forearm (a so-called *wrist coach*) so that we can see the adjustments directly when we are at the shooting station, or see game that we intend to shoot. If we do not know exactly what distances we will shoot at, which is often the case in various forms of long-range shooting and hunting, it is wise to note wind adjustments at different distances for the two wind speeds we have measured. An alternative is to have ready-made tables with different wind intervals that we can choose depending on the base winds that prevail, such as for example 2-7 m/s, 8-13 m/s and so on.

By the time we're competing or hunting, we already have a good idea of the prevailing wind speeds and can concentrate more on range finding or shooting technique. When shooting, we can look directly at the vegetation we have previously observed and get an idea of how the current wind speed relates to the measured base winds. Since the various adjustments are readily available, we can either use any of them directly, or assess how the wind deviates from the observed base winds, in order to change the adjustments accordingly.

Just be mindful that we also have to assess the angle of the crosswind to the trajectory, in order to determine the crosswind effect. This can be done with the kind of tool that I have appended in the end of this book. Field shooting or PRS, when shooting at unknown distances with the wind coming from different angles, requires that the angle of the wind be taken into account for each individual shooting station. This does not have to be done with extreme accuracy. In practice, it is often possible to determine the wind angle to the trajectory with a margin of error of about +/- 5 degrees. But as usual, the rule for shooting is that the more accurate we are when measuring and adjusting, the better the result. Nowadays there are special anemometers that can be turned to determine the angle of the wind in relation to the trajectory, but an old proven trick is the *cassette tape method*. I've never heard anyone use this term, but I've seen a number of older and more experienced shooters use it, so I'm coining the term. The plastic bands inside cassette tapes are extremely light, and move with the wind at the slightest wind speed. If we attach a meter or so of such a tape to a small box or equivalent, we can pick it up when we are facing the target, hold it up with an outstretched arm, and let the tape move with the wind. In this way, it is easier to see the exact angle of the tape to the line of sight to the target. Once we have both an estimated wind speed and an estimated angle to the target, we can make the necessary adjustments and shoot.

The great advantage of the low-high method is that we have a relatively good understanding of the wind situation already when we get to our shooting site. We don't have to waste time measuring the wind speed when shooting, but instead focus on other aspects of the shot. Another advantage is the speed of implementation of wind compensation. Since we already have a good idea of what adjustments will be involved in the shot, we can focus on fine tuning rather than coarse adjustment, which gives a more accurate result on the target.

Split the distance

Another method for wind compensation is to divide the distance between us and the target, analyze one piece at a time, and then combine them to get an overall picture. This method is more appropriate at very long distances, and is therefore better suited to competitive shooters in very long-range disciplines such as Precision Rifle Series (PRS) or F class. The number of sections we divide the range into depends on the distance. If we are shooting at 1000 meters/1100 yards, we can divide the range into at least two parts and look at each part separately. If we are shooting at even longer distances, we can divide the range into three parts.

There is a competition in the USA called "King of 2 miles" where they shoot at distances as long as two American miles, i.e. about 3.2 kilometers. When the shooters participating in the competition are interviewed, it is sometimes heard that they divide the distance into three roughly equal sections and evaluate each section separately, then add up the expected drift and decide what adjustments need to be made. To assess the wind at different sections of the trajectory, long range-shooters sometimes use mirage, according to the method described below.

Mirage

Mirage is the name of the thermal radiation that can be seen rising from the ground, especially on hot summer days. Most people recognize the phenomenon from looking at a hot asphalt road in the summer. In physical terms, mirage is an optical phenomenon perceived when light passes through layers of air with different temperatures and densities. The air closer to the ground has a higher temperature and lower density than the air above it. The different density of the air layers gives light passing through the air a slightly different angle of refraction, and we perceive it as the air quivering. The same thing happens, for example, when light passes between air and a water surface, but the refraction of the light is more predictable because the light is refracted between two different media. In the case of different layers of air, the refraction of light is not as definite or abrupt, and therefore the phenomenon is perceived more as a trembling in the air or that the air seems to swing back and forth.

The reason why the phenomenon is so often observed on highways, for example, is that the road absorbs a lot of solar energy and heats up the air layer above it considerably. This creates a greater temperature difference in the air layers above the road, and in turn produces a much stronger optical effect. Mirage can potentially exist all year round, but in colder countries it is not so easy to see in the colder seasons. The effect is often so small when it is cold outside that it is not perceived by the eye. When we are on the shooting range shooting multiple series, the barrel heats the air layer above it in front of the rifle scope, which makes it look like the target is dancing through the scope, and it can be difficult to get a focused sight picture. For this reason, it is common to have a so-called mirage band over the barrel, the task of which is to direct the heat radiation away from the line of sight. Suppressors are another part that often gets hot, and causes mirage in front of the scope. There are suppressor jackets made of special heat-absorbing materials that can partially remedy the problem.

So, what does mirage have to do with shooting? Many shooters use mirage as a tool, to assess the direction and strength of the wind. Mirage is primarily useful for assessing wind direction, and only secondarily for assessing wind speed. When we look at the mirage, we analyze how it moves, and whether the "waves" caused by the mirage appear to go straight up or whether they veer off to the right or left. When the mirage rises straight up toward the sky, it is said that it is boiling, and this means that there is hardly any wind. Some people use the mirage to judge wind speed, but this is not a very accurate method because it takes a wind speed of only about 5-6 meters per second (11-13 mph) for the mirage to be horizontal. For this reason, it is not very useful for determining the speed of stronger winds. For competition purposes, it is better to have an electronic anemometer. However, it can be useful to use the mirage to look for the direction of the wind in relation to the trajectory. To do this, we can use binoculars or a spotting scope to look toward the target in order to see which way the mirage is "leaning". When looking at the target, we then turn our body in the direction from which the wind is blowing from and keep looking in the binoculars until we perceive that the mirage is rising straight up without leaning. This is the direction from which the wind is blowing. The mirage no longer tilts to one side because we observe the mirage between ourselves and the direction from which the wind is blowing. The wind thus blows straight toward us. By estimating the angle between that direction and the position of the target, we can then go on to calculate the crosswind effect. In order to see the mirage clearly, it is necessary to focus the rifle scope or spotting scope on the air between the shooter and the target, rather than only on the target. If the trajectory is divided up into several parts and assessed separately, we need to change the optical focus to capture the mirage at different parts of the trajectory. This method can be used to discover whether there are conflicting crosswinds along the trajectory.

Aerodynamic jump

What is sometimes called aerodynamic jump is the vertical component of wind drift, i.e. the vertical drift caused by a crosswind. This is basically due to the same mechanism as the gyroscopic drift, which will be discussed in detail below. The projectile, when gyroscopically stabilized, reacts by turning 90 degrees to the force acting on it. In the case of a crosswind, the projectile reacts by turning slightly upward or downward when affected by wind from the right or left in the direction of the shot. The size of the aerodynamic jump varies with the wind speed, and the length of time the projectile is affected by the wind. This vertical wind drift is typically very small, and in most cases nothing to be concerned about. However, when shooting at very long distances, it can cause a noticeable drift.

The above definition of aerodynamic jump is the most common. But sometimes when aerodynamic jump is mentioned, it refers to a small change of direction that the bullet can make when it passes from the barrel to traveling freely in the air, which strictly speaking does not concern external ballistics but transition ballistics. There can be a number of causes for this type of aerodynamic jump: a strong cross wind, inconsistencies in the material of the bullet, inconsistencies in the crowning of the barrel, or a muzzle brake or suppressor. In this way, the bullet can "jump" in its trajectory as it leaves the barrel and begins to travel freely in the air.

Headwind or tailwind

Headwind or tailwind affects the air resistance encountered by the bullet. A tailwind means that the bullet encounters less air resistance, and thus maintains its velocity better. Therefore, it will have less time to be affected by gravity over a given distance and will be pulled less towards the ground. This means that we hit high when shooting downwind. On the contrary, we hit low when shooting into a headwind, because the bullet encounters more air resistance and loses velocity faster. The effect of head- and tailwind on the trajectory is generally negligible at short and medium distances for a given caliber, but at the end of the trajectory it can have a significant effect on a projectile. The size of the effect is of course related to the strength of the wind, and also to the ballistic coefficient of the projectile. A bullet with a lower ballistic coefficient will be more affected by the change in air resistance than a bullet with a higher ballistic coefficient. Below are tables with some examples of how headwind and tailwind affect the bullet trajectory of a 6.5 mm projectile at different ranges.

Headwind and tailwind

Table 33: 6.5x55 mm tailwind (Metric)

- 130 gn (8.42 grams) match bullet
- BC (G7): 0.274
- 900 m/s (2950 fps) muzzle velocity
- 15° C (59° F)
- Air pressure 1015 hPa
- Relative humidity 40 %.

		Wind speed (m/s)		
		(no wind)	2 m/s	4 m/s
D	100	6	6	6
I	200	26	26	26
S	300	62	62	62
T	400	117	116	116
A	500	192	191	190
N	600	293	291	289
C	700	422	419	417
E	800	585	581	577
	900	788	782	777
(m)	1000	1037	1029	1021

Absolute bullet drop (cm)

Table 34: 6.5x55 mm tailwind (Imperial)

Table 34 is based on the same parameters as table 33.

		(no wind)	Wind speed (mph)	
		(no wind)	5 mph	10 mph
D	100	2.1	2.1	2.1
I	200	8.7	8.6	8.6
S	300	20.4	20.3	20.1
T	400	37.8	37.6	37.4
A	500	62	61.6	61.2
N	600	93	92	92.4
C	700	134	133	132
E	800	184	182	181
	900	246	244	242
(yd)	1000	321	319	316

Absolute bullet drop (inches)

Table 35: 6.5x55 mm headwind (Metric)

Table 35 is based on the same parameters as table 33.

		(no wind)	Wind speed (m/s)	
		(no wind)	2 m/s	4 m/s
D	100	6	6	6
I	200	26	27	27
S	300	62	63	63
T	400	117	118	118
A	500	192	194	195
N	600	293	295	296
C	700	422	425	427
E	800	585	589	593
	900	788	793	799
(m)	1000	1037	1045	1053

Absolute bullet drop (cm)

Table 36: 6.5x55 mm headwind (Imperial)

Table 36 is based on the same parameters as table 33.

| | | Wind speed (mph) | | |
		(no wind)	5 mph	10 mph
D	100	2.1	2.1	2.1
I	200	8.7	8.7	8.7
S	300	20.4	20.5	20.6
T	400	37.8	38.0	38.3
A	500	62.0	62.4	62.7
N	600	93	94.1	94.7
C	700	134	134	135
E	800	184	185	186
	900	246	247	249
(yd)	1000	321	324	327

Absolute bullet drop (inches)

As shown in the tables above, the effect of head- and tailwinds at short to medium distances is negligible, causing only a few centimeters of vertical dispersion (less than one inch) at 500 meters (≅ 550 yd). However, at the end of the trajectory, a much greater impact is noted. At 900 meters there is an 11 cm (4.3") difference between no wind and 4 m/s tailwind, and at 1000 meters about 16 cm or 6.3". The implication of this is that we do not need to take into account head- and tailwind in normal hunting and shooting situations, but only for example in long-range precision shooting.

Vertical winds

Because terrain usually moves up and down, there is usually a vertical wind component in wind, even if it is not very big. The strength of the vertical wind component depends on the topography of the terrain. The greater the difference between high points and low points in the terrain, the greater the vertical wind component. Since the angle of repose of ordinary ground is usually no greater than 30 degrees in nature, this means that the vertical wind component will be relatively small. Shooting in mountainous terrain is quite different, and for longer shots in mountainous terrain it may be necessary to pay extra attention to this phenomenon. When a wind blows against mountainsides, there is always a vertical component whose effect on the projectile trajectory is relative to the wind speed, and which at very long distances can affect a bullet trajectory significantly. A projectile imparted with drift from a vertical wind at the beginning of the trajectory, will continue to drift from the intended trajectory.

Wind gradient

Wind speed increases with increasing height. This is because the air closer to the ground has a higher density and weight, and therefore moves more slowly, and there is friction between the air and the vegetation on the ground, as well as buildings. This means that wind cannot have the same speed at lower altitudes, and also that the shape of the ground and vegetation can channel the wind and change its direction. The shape of the ground is very important. All surfaces reduce wind speed, but they do so to varying degrees. For example, a wind is about 20-30% weaker at the surface of a lake compared to the wind speed a few hundred meters up, but the reduction in speed can be as much as 40-50% for areas with vegetation, or in an urban environment. The increase in wind strength is not predetermined exactly, but occurs gradually and starts at ground level. This means that the wind is a little stronger one meter above the ground than 50 cm above the ground, even stronger two meters up, and so on.

Wind gradient, also called wind speed gradient, is the term for the increasing speed of the wind with height. A small wind gradient means that the wind increases less with increasing height, and a large wind gradient means that it increases more with increasing height. Wind gradient is central when planning the placement of wind turbines for example, but it can also be useful to understand for shooting at long distances, or in different environments such as mountains or cities. Mountain or urban environments are obviously not environments that competition shooters usually shoot in, but are more relevant to military or police snipers. Of course, hunting also occurs in mountainous environments, and for those involved in hunting in mountains it can be useful to have an understanding of wind gradient.

It is usually not necessary to consider, or compensate for, wind gradient in normal shooting conditions over flat ground, but in some situations, it may be necessary to be aware of it. Examples of this are shooting between hills, mountains or off of mountain sides. The wind may have a low speed on the hill where we are shooting and a low speed at the hill where the target is located, but still a much higher speed between the hills which can lead to missing the target. This is because the bullet trajectory between the hills is higher above ground level than both the shooting location and the target. As wind speed increases with height, the wind between the hills has a higher speed, and the higher the hills are, the greater the variation in wind speed will be. Shooting off a slope or hillside can be treacherous, as the wind speed may be low at the firing point and at the target, but much higher just off the slope we are shooting from. This is quite a common situation in long range shooting competitions, and can throw beginning shooters off.

When calculating the wind gradient, there is a variable in the formula that denotes the roughness of the ground, i.e., the type of surface over which the wind gradient is to be calculated. Below is a table of different soil types that have different *roughness measures.*

The roughness measure indicates how easily the air moves through the different types of terrain, and thus how slowly or rapidly the wind speed increases with height. The lower the number, the easier it is for the air to move, such as over a still body of water, which means the least friction for the air. Large cities with skyscrapers provide the most friction for the air, and therefore the wind generally increases more slowly with increasing height there.

Table 37: Roughness measurements

Type of land	Roughness measure
Water surface	0
Open terrain with a smooth surface, e.g. airfield, mowed grass.	0.5
Open farmland with no fences or hedges and very few buildings. Only gently rounded hills.	1
Agricultural land with a few buildings and high hedges or trees with about 1250 meters between them (very sparse farms).	1.5
Agricultural land with a few buildings and high hedges or trees spaced about 500 meters apart (sparse farms).	2
Agricultural land with many buildings, shrubs, plants and tall hedges or trees with about 250 meters between them.	2.5
Villages, small towns, farmland with many or tall trees and hedges, forests and very hilly and uneven terrain.	3
Larger cities with tall buildings	3.5
Big cities with tall buildings and skyscrapers	4

GYROSCOPIC STABILIZATION

The chapter after this one discusses the phenomenon of gyroscopic drift and its importance to rifle shooting, but first we will discuss gyroscopic stabilization in general, what it is, and why it matters. When a rifle bullet is pushed by the propellant gases through the barrel of a rifle, it is forced to rotate by the rifling in the barrel. The lands in the barrel engage the bullet's jacket and cause the bullet to rotate. *Twist rate* is a term used to describe the distance at which the rifling in the barrel rotates a full revolution inside the barrel. The twist rate is given as "1: nr of inches", where 1 means one full revolution in the barrel and the number of inches is the distance at which the rifling completes the full revolution. On most hunting rifles, the twist rate is somewhere between 1:9 and 1:12. This means that the lands in the barrel rotate a full revolution at a distance of between 9 and 12 inches. In metric terms, this is 1:22.86 cm and 1:30.48 cm respectively.

Twist rate is often referred to as *fast* or *slow*. A faster twist rate means that the lands make a full rotation in the barrel at a shorter distance. This forces the bullet to rotate faster for a given muzzle velocity. Conversely, a slower twist rate means that the bullet is given a slower rotational speed. In this way, 1:9 is said to be a faster twist rate than 1:12. There is no qualitative value in this statement; the 1:9 twist rate is not inherently better than 1:12. It is merely more suitable for a particular combination of caliber, bullet weight and muzzle velocity.

When we think about twist rate in general, at first glance it doesn't seem that extreme. A bullet that is forced to rotate one revolution in 30 centimeters (12 inches) does not seem very fast. It only appears extreme when we consider that the average hunting bullet travels around 830 meters per second (2700 fps). This means that the bullet rotates at an initial speed of 2760 revolutions per second. The centrifugal forces developed at this rotational speed are enormous, and a projectile fired in a weapon with a much faster twist rate than it was designed for can be torn apart in flight by centrifugal force. In accordance with American tradition, the rotation of the bullet is clockwise when viewed from the shooter's perspective. In contrast, the British had a tradition of rifling the barrels counterclockwise from the shooter. There was a theory that this would help compensate for the tendency of right-handed shooters to pull to the right when firing, which in turn affects the bullet trajectory. It is unclear if this notion is based on any empirical data. In general, tradition seems to dictate that most rifles have the rifling clockwise as seen from the receiver of the rifle.

Gyroscopic stabilization is based on the physical phenomenon that a rotating object tends to resist changes in direction of its axis of rotation. If elongated rifle bullets are not gyroscopically stabilized, they tend to rotate about themselves longitudinally rather than about their longitudinal axis (spin). If we were to load a bullet that is too long for a particular caliber into our gun and shoot it, we could end up with an elongated bullet hole in the target because the bullet did not have enough rotational speed to stabilize gyroscopically, and therefore hit the target sideways. This is a problem partly because the bullet loses its aerodynamic properties in flight when it flies sideways, and partly because it becomes unpredictable in flight and also loses its terminal ballistic properties.

The general rule is that the longer a bullet is in relation to the caliber, i.e., the diameter of the barrel, the faster it must rotate to stabilize. This also usually means that the heavier a bullet is for its caliber, the faster it needs to rotate, since a heavier bullet in a given caliber is usually also longer than a lighter one. Sometimes the box for the bullets states the twist rate the bullets need to stabilize. This is of course important information, but normally nothing to worry about since most hunting rifles can stabilize the most common bullet weights in the specific caliber with some margin. However, it is all the more important if we are building a match rifle from scratch, and thinking about what twist rate we need for a particular bullet we have decided that we want to shoot.

Contrary to popular belief, the aerodynamic stability of the bullet increases during the flight towards the target. This is because the *velocity of the bullet decreases much faster than the rotational speed of the bullet*, and it is the air resistance that creates instability in bullets. However, the transonic transition may destabilize the bullet again in the end of the trajectory, if the shot is very long for the caliber.

In Figure 14 below is a projectile with its imaginary axis of rotation going straight through it. As the bullet rotates, it is more difficult to change the angle of the bullet, because the mass of the bullet is in motion around its own longitudinal axis.

Figure 14: axis of rotation of the bullet

However, the gyroscopic stabilization also gives rise to some undesirable effects. When a projectile is fired at long range, the barrel is inclined upward and so is the tip of the bullet. After some time in flight, the bullet has reached its highest point and starts to fall downward in its trajectory due to gravity. But the bullet's gyroscopic stabilization tends to preserve the angle of the bullet's axis of rotation, so the tip of the bullet continues to point upward even as the bullet turns downward in its trajectory towards its target. When falling towards the target, the bullet corrects its own general angle in the air as dictated by air resistance; the tip of the bullet begins to point downward toward the target because the surface friction from the air forces it to do so. Thus, two opposing forces are observed: the tip of the bullet tends to point upward, but the surface friction from the air changes the angle towards the target as it descends in its trajectory. The friction from the air does not completely overcome the gyroscopic stability of the bullet. Even when the bullet drops downward in its trajectory towards the target, it has the tip pointing slightly upward.

Gyroscopic drift

Gyroscopic drift (often called spin drift) means that the bullet tends to drift in the same direction as it rotates. The gyroscopic drift is, for most rifles, insignificant at short and medium distances, but quickly becomes noticeable as the projectile approaches the end of its trajectory. This means that gyroscopic drift is of interest primarily to sport shooters and hunters who shoot at longer distances, as well as military snipers. Hunters who hunt at shorter distances do not need to consider gyroscopic drift. When shooting at very long distances for a given caliber, the gyroscopic drift increases significantly. This is because the velocity of the projectile is significantly lower at those distances, while the rotation of the projectile has not decreased proportionally with the velocity. This means that we get a relatively more significant gyroscopic drift when the projectile is at the end of its trajectory.

For instance, a 140 gn 6.5 Creedmoor match bullet shot 800 meters (875 yd) from a 1:8 twist barrel will drift approximately 7.3 cm or about 3". The same bullet will, at a 1000 meter (1100 yd) shot, drift 15 cm or about 6". This example serves to illustrate how gyroscopic drift increases rapidly in the end of the trajectory. This is very important to consider in long-range shooting, and of course applies to all calibers.

The tables below exemplify gyroscopic drift for some common calibers. The examples are intended to provide a general understanding of the significance of gyroscopic drift, and not to be understood as fixed drift numbers for certain calibers. The precise gyroscopic drift of any projectile depends on many variables. The parameters of the examples below include the value of the *gyroscopic stability factor*, which is a measure of how stable a projectile is in flight. We will look later in the chapter in detail at how to calculate the gyroscopic stability factor.

Tables gyroscopic drift

Table 38: 6.5x55 mm

- 130 gn (8.42 grams) match bullet
- BC (G7): 0.274
- 900 m/s (2950 fps) muzzle velocity
- Bullet length: 35 mm
- Twist rate: 1:220 mm (8.66 inches, the usual rate for the standard competition weapon in caliber 6.5x55 mm, Sauer STR 200)
- Temperature: 15° C (59° F)
- Zeroing distance: 300 meters
- Gyroscopic stability factor: 1.36

Distance in m (yd)	Gyroscopic drift in cm (inches) to the right in the shooting direction
500 m ($\cong$550 yd)	2.6 cm (1")
600 m	4 cm
700 m	7 cm
800 m ($\cong$875 yd)	10 cm (3.9")
900 m	14 cm
1000 m	19 cm
1100 m	25 cm
1200 m ($\cong$1300 yd)	32 cm (12.5")

In the example above, we assume that the weapon was sighted in at 300 meters which is commonplace for competition rifles in caliber 6.5x55 mm. As can be seen from Table 38, the gyroscopic drift is small when shooting up to about 500-600 meters. After that, it is not insignificant and increases rapidly, and can lead to missing a target in competition.

Table 39: 6.5 Creedmoor

- 140 gn (9.07 grams) match bullet
- BC (G7): 0.304
- 820 m/s (2690 fps) muzzle velocity
- Bullet length: 35.2 mm
- Twist rate: 1:8
- Temperature: 15° C (59° F)
- Zeroing distance: 300 meters
- Gyroscopic stability factor: 1.66

Distance in m (yd)	Gyroscopic drift in cm (inches) to the right in the shooting direction
500 m ($\cong$550 yd)	1.1 cm (0.4")
600 m	2.5 cm
700 m	4.5 cm
800 m ($\cong$875 yd)	7.3 cm (2.9")
900 m	10.9 cm
1000 m	15.6 cm
1100 m	21.7 cm
1200 m ($\cong$1300 yd)	29.2 cm (11.4")

Let's look at an example with a caliber designed for long range shooting: .338 Lapua Magnum. The parameters in the example below are based on a 250 gn Lapua Scenar bullet.

Table 40: .338 Lapua Magnum

- 250 gn (16.2 grams) match bullet
- BC (G7): 0.322
- 905 m/s (2970 fps) muzzle velocity
- Bullet length: 39.49 mm
- Twist rate: 1:11
- Temperature: 15° C (59° F)
- Zeroing distance: 300 meters
- Gyroscopic stability factor: 1.84

Distance in m (yd)	Gyroscopic drift in cm (inches) to the right in the shooting direction
500 m (≅550 yd)	3 cm (1.2")
600 m	5 cm
700 m	7 cm
800 m (≅875 yd)	11 cm (4.3")
900 m	15 cm
1000 m	19 cm
1100 m (≅1200 yd)	26 cm (10.2")
1200 m	33 cm
1300 m	41 cm
1400 m (≅1530 yd)	51 cm (20")
1500 m	63 cm
1600 m	77 cm
1700 m (≅1860 yd)	93 cm (36")

The twist rate in the above example is 1:11, which is common for the .338 Lapua Magnum. The bullet weighing 16.2 grams with this twist rate has a gyroscopic stability factor of 1.84, which is higher than in the examples with 6.5x55 mm and 6.5 Creedmoor, and thus leads to a slightly larger gyroscopic drift. The drift is small at medium distances, but beyond that we need to be aware of the drift. Suppose a military sniper were to try to engage a target at 1400 meters with this caliber, which is a realistic scenario. If the shooter then fails to compensate for gyroscopic drift, he will probably miss to the side of the target. To sum up, gyroscopic drift is insignificant at short and medium distances, and depending on the caliber possibly even longer than that, but quickly becomes noticeable when the projectile is at the end of its trajectory. This means that gyroscopic drift is of interest primarily to sport shooters and hunters who shoot at longer distances, as well as military snipers.

The mechanism of gyroscopic drift

As observed earlier, when we looked at the bullet's axis of rotation and gyroscopic stability, the tip of the bullet tends to point upward even when it is heading downward in its trajectory toward the target. This results in a force caused by the combination of air resistance and the downward trajectory of the bullet, acting against the tip of the bullet and trying to push it upward. The picture below represents the phenomenon known as the *overturning force*. The arrow represents the air resistance.

Figure 15: upward angle of the bullet

The angle of the bullet is known as *angle of attack*. Since the bullet in the air is angled slightly upward, while being pulled downward by gravity, air resistance acts to rotate the bullet upward and backward. When force is applied to the axis of a rotating object, the axis tends to move not in the direction in which the force is applied, but at a right angle to it. The direction in which the axis rotates (yaws) depends on the direction of rotation of the projectile. The principle is the same as putting a spinning top in rotation on a table. When we apply force to the center axis of the spinning top, it will not move in the direction the force was applied, but perpendicular to it.

Figure 16 below shows a projectile from the front. The arrow below the bullet represents the overturning force that tries to rotate the bullet upward. The arrow pointing to the left represents how the tip of the bullet responds by moving. The bullet in the picture is rotating clockwise, as seen from the shooter.

Figure 16: gyroscopic drift

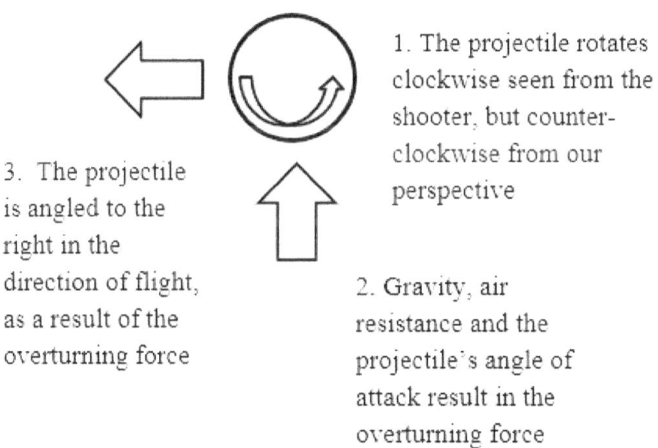

If the direction of rotation of the bullet had instead been counter-clockwise, the gyroscopic drift would have been to the left in the direction of fire. Since the axis of the bullet is imparted a slight angle to the side, this causes a slight change of course from the trajectory towards the target that the bullet was on. The resulting angle is very small, usually less than 0.1 degrees, which means that the effect of gyroscopic drift is relatively small, but as we have seen, it must still be taken into account at long and very long distances. *The gyroscopic drift becomes greater the longer we shoot, the faster the projectile rotates and the higher the density of the air.* Gyroscopic drift is also to some extent countered by the general drag of the projectile. When the bullet is angled in the same direction as the direction of rotation, the air resistance causes it to be pushed in the opposite direction across the line of sight in the same way as wind drift. This effect is relatively small, due to a couple of factors. Firstly, the gyroscopic drift is greatest at the end of the bullet's trajectory and thus does not affect the shot to the same extent during the entire projectile trajectory, and secondly, the projectile has a lower velocity and thus encounters less air resistance than earlier during the projectile trajectory.

Overstabilization

Above we have discussed the effect of gyroscopic stabilization on the bullet, as well as the twist rate of the rifle barrel. We have also mentioned the gyroscopic stability factor, which is an estimate of how stable the bullet is in flight. This brings us to the issue of overstabilization.

It is possible to have an inappropriately fast, i.e. short, twist rate in a barrel. The faster the twist rate, the faster the bullet rotates for a given velocity. A faster twist rate makes the bullet's gyroscopic stabilization stronger and harder to break, which means that the bullet will resist being angled downward towards the target, leading to a stronger overturning force. As we have seen, this increases the gyroscopic drift.

Thus, there needs to be a balance between the gyroscopic drift and the aerodynamic stability of the bullet. The bullet should be stable enough to retain its orientation and aerodynamic properties in the air, but should not have such a high rotational speed that it causes excessive gyroscopic drift. A projectile can thus be considered too stable, and cause more gyroscopic drift than necessary. This phenomenon is called overstabilization. Another and more extreme effect of overstabilization of bullets is when the bullet rotates so fast that it tears apart in flight. This can happen, for instance, if we attempt to shoot under-calibrated ammunition in rifles, and the projectiles are not built to withstand the centrifugal force that develops when they are fired. An example of this is when we shoot some .223 caliber bullets at extremely high velocities using a sabot[17] in a .30 caliber rifle. The bullet simply does not have the tensile strength to withstand the centrifugal forces and is torn apart. This is of course an extreme example and not something we would normally care about, but it highlights the fact that stabilizing the bullet is a balancing act that has both pros and cons, and that we need to know what we are doing when determining the rifling pitch of a gun, as well as taking into account which projectiles are to be fired from the rifle. This is not a consideration that ordinary hunters, who usually buy off-the-shelf rifles, need to make, but is something that professional gunsmiths need to consider when building weapons.

---

[17] A sabot is a device the keeps a projectile centered in a barrel of larger diameter. A sabot is typically used in ammunition for heavier military guns, but can also be used in small arms to increase the velocity of the projectile. There are military sniper rifles that make use of sabots to fire tungsten sub-caliber projectiles with extremely high velocity.

Calculation of gyroscopic drift

Modern ballistic calculators and applications can of course calculate gyroscopic drift without any problem. I have included the equation to illustrate for the mathematically interested reader. The equations I have seen for this purpose give the answer in inches, but for shooters in Europe I have modified one such equation to provide the drift in cm as well.

$$Gyroscopic\ drift\ in\ cm\ =\ 3.175(Sg + 1.2)tof^{1.83}$$

In which:

3.175 = the constant that gives the gives in cm. Using 1.25 instead gives the drift in inches.

Sg = the gyroscopic stability factor according to the *Miller twist rule*.[18] Later in this chapter there is a description of how to calculate the gyroscopic stability factor for a particular bullet and barrel combination. There is also an excellent calculator for this particular parameter on the Berger Bullet website, which we can use to avoid having to calculate the gyroscopic stability factor ourselves. Some ballistic calculators also calculate the stability factor automatically when we enter the values for a particular projectile and velocity.

1.2 = another constant to be included.

---

[18] Rule developed by Don Miller to predict the correct rifling of barrels. Miller also developed an equation to assess the gyroscopic stability of a bullet.

tof = *time of flight*, i.e., the flight time of the bullet at the distance for which we want to calculate the drift.

1.83 = constant exponent.

Remember that we do not need to include the distance at which we have zeroed our weapon when calculating gyroscopic drift. This is because we have already compensated for that small amount of drift when we zeroed the rifle. When we subtract the zeroing distance from the total gyroscopic drift, we do so by calculating the drift at the zeroing range and subtracting it from the drift at the longer range. If we subtract the *time of flight* rather than the absolute drift we introduce an error in the calculation, as the same time of flight at different distances results in different gyroscopic drifts, because of the varying velocity of the bullet during the trajectory.

Gyroscopic stability factor

The American Don Miller developed formulas to find the optimum twist rate to stabilize a bullet of a certain weight. One of his formulas gives what is called the gyroscopic stability factor (Sg), also known as the gyroscopic stability coefficient. So, Sg is not a constant in the equation for calculating gyroscopic drift, but varies depending on which bullet we want to calculate the drift for. Miller's equation is slightly more complicated than the equation for calculating the gyroscopic drift. To avoid calculating it ourselves manually, we can use Berger Bullet's calculator available on their website. Some better ballistic applications for mobile phones can also provide this information, but it is not obvious which formula they use to calculate the value. Below is the formula to calculate it ourselves:

$$Sg = \frac{30m}{t^2 d^3 l(1 + l^2)}$$

In which:

Sg = gyroscopic stability factor.

m = bullet weight in grains (gn)

t = barrel twist rate measured in number of calibers per revolution. Caliber means the actual caliber of the weapon being calculated, in inches. For a 7.62 mm, that is 0.30 inches.

d = diameter of the bullet in inches

l = length of the bullet in calibers

THE CORIOLIS AND EÖTVÖS EFFECTS

When reading about the Coriolis effect, we often see two different names - the *Coriolis force* and the *Coriolis effect*. The Coriolis force is the name of the force itself, and the Coriolis effect is its effects on moving objects. To complicate things a bit, the Coriolis force is not an actual force such as gravity or electromagnetic force. Instead, the Coriolis force is itself a result of living on a rotating sphere, and is therefore sometimes referred to as a 'fictitious force' or 'apparent force'. But because its effects are real, no matter how we characterize the nature of the force, and it is described as a force in scientific contexts, I do so in this book as well. The Coriolis effect is practically negligible for rifle shooting at short and medium ranges, but it can become a concern at very long ranges, depending on the shooter's geographical location.

The Coriolis force is an effect of the Earth's rotation, and it consists of a vertical and a horizontal component. Horizontal meaning that it causes the projectile to drift sideways relative to the line of sight and the target, thus affecting lateral dispersion. The vertical component of course causes vertical dispersion. The two forces have different physical mechanisms and are thus different forces, but since they are both effects of the Earth's rotation, they are usually lumped together and called the "Coriolis effect" together. The vertical component of the Coriolis effect also has its own name and is called the *Eötvös effect*. Both of these effects will be discussed in detail in this chapter. Below is the Coriolis effect summarized.

The horizontal component:

- The Coriolis force causes all projectiles traveling a longer distance in the northern hemisphere to drift to the right as seen from the shooter, *regardless of the direction in which they are fired.*
- Conversely, the Coriolis force causes all projectiles traveling a longer distance in the southern hemisphere to drift to the left as seen from the shooter, *regardless of the direction in which they are fired.*
- The horizontal component of the Coriolis force is strongest at the poles and weakest at the Equator. This means that it has a greater impact the further north or south of the Equator we shoot. It has a negligible effect at the Equator on projectiles traveling to the north or south. When shooting east or west at the Equator, it has no effect at all.

The vertical component - the Eötvös effect:

- The Eötvös effect causes projectiles fired east to move upward in their trajectory and hit high in the target if not compensated for.
- Conversely, the Eötvös effect causes projectiles fired west to hit lower than intended if not compensated for.
- In contrast to the horizontal component of the Coriolis effect, the Eötvös effect is strongest at the Equator and non-existent precisely at the poles.
- The Eötvös effect has the biggest effect on the trajectory when shooting *straight* to the east or west, but it also has a lesser effect when shooting at angles east or west, such as

northwest or southwest. Thus, unlike the horizontal component of the Coriolis effect, the Eötvös effect is *directionally sensitive*, something that needs to be accounted for when compensating for it.

The good thing about the Coriolis effect is that it is completely predictable. As long as we know where we are on Earth, how far we are shooting, and in which direction we are shooting, we can compensate accurately for the Coriolis effect. There are formulas for calculating the Coriolis effect and the Eötvös effect which are presented below, and we will also discuss the physical mechanisms of these forces in more detail.

The horizontal component of the Coriolis effect is mathematically a function of (1) how fast the Earth is spinning, (2) the distance to the target, (3) the latitude of the shooter, and (4) the time it takes for the projectile to reach the target.

Coriolis drift

The Coriolis effect is completely negligible at normal hunting distances, and typically also at medium and long distances. At very long distances, and especially closer to the North or South Pole, the horizontal component may need to be accounted for, depending on the precision requirements of the shot. Closer to the equator, the Eötvös drift may have to be accounted for when shooting east or west.

For instance, a 6.5x55 Swede shot at 500 meters at the 59th parallel North (i.e., Alaska, central Canada or southern Sweden) will drift about 2 cm (0.78") to the right. The same load at a 1000-meter shot will drift about 10 cm (4") inches to the right. At 500 meters the Coriolis drift is pretty much negligible, but at 1000 meters it can be significant in a precision shooting event. In contrast, the same load shot 500 and 1000 meters at the latitude of Mexico City will change point of impact 0.8 cm (0.31") and 3.9 cm (1.5") to the right respectively, highlighting the difference in horizontal Coriolis drift between latitudes.

In regards to the vertical Coriolis drift (Eötvös effect), a 6.5 Creedmoor shot 1000 meters straight to the east (45 degrees) at the 59th parallel will cause the bullet to rise 8 cm, and cause it to sink exactly the same amount in its trajectory if shot straight to the west. In contrast, the same load shot 1000 meters to the east at the Equator will cause a projectile rise of 15 cm, i.e., almost the double, and cause it to sink exactly the same amount in its trajectory if shot straight to the west.

Below is a set of ballistic tables that are intended to give the reader a general idea about the Coriolis and Eötvös effects on projectile trajectories. In the examples below, the gyroscopic drift is excluded, so that the Coriolis drift can be isolated.

Horizontal Coriolis drift North

The examples below assume that we are shooting at the 59th parallel north, i.e., the latitude of Alaska, central Canada or southern Sweden. This is approximately 1000 km (600 miles) south of the Arctic Circle. Thus, the drift in the tables below refer to drift to the right in the direction of shooting.

Table 41: 6.5x55

- 130 gn (8.42 grams) match bullet
- BC (G7): 0.274
- 900 m/s (2950 fps) muzzle velocity

Distance in m (yd)	Horizontal Coriolis drift in cm (inches)
500 m (546 yd)	2 cm (0.78")
600 m	3 cm
700 m (765 yd)	4.2 cm (1.65")
800 m	5.8 cm
900 m (984 yd)	7.8 cm (3.0")
1000 m	10 cm
1100 m (1202 yd)	12.7 cm (5")
1200 m	15.8 cm

Table 42: 6.5 Creedmoor

- 140 gn (9.07 grams) match bullet
- BC (G7): 0.304
- 820 m/s (2690 fps) muzzle velocity

Distance in m (yd)	Horizontal Coriolis drift in cm (inches)
500 m (546 yd)	1.5 cm (0.6")
600 m	2.6 cm
700 m (765 yd)	4 cm (1.57")
800 m	5.7 cm
900 m (984 yd)	7.8 cm (3.0")
1000 m	10.2 cm
1100 m (1202 yd)	13.1 cm (5.1")
1200 m	16.5 cm

Table 43: .308 Winchester

- 168 gn (10.89 grams) match bullet
- BC (G7): 0.218
- 808 m/s (2650 fps) muzzle velocity

Distance in m (yd)	Horizontal Coriolis drift in cm (inches)
500 m (546 yd)	2.4 cm (0.9")
600 m	3.7 cm
700 m (765 yd)	5.3 cm (2.0")
800 m	7.4 cm
900 m (984 yd)	10 cm (3.9")
1000 m	13 cm
1100 m (1202 yd)	16.6 cm (6.5")
1200 m	20.7 cm

Table 44: .338 Lapua Magnum

- 250 gn (16.2 grams) match bullet
- BC (G7): 0.322
- 905 m/s (2970 fps) muzzle velocity

Distance in m (yd)	Horizontal Coriolis drift in cm (inches)
800 m (874 yd)	5.5 cm (2.1")
900 m	7.3 cm
1000 m (1093 yd)	9.4 cm (3.7")
1100 m	11.9 cm
1200 m (1312 yd)	14.6 cm (5.7")
1300 m	17.8 cm
1400 m (1531 yd)	21.6 cm (8.5")
1500 m	26 cm
1600 m (1749 yd)	30.8 cm (12.1")
1700 m	36.1 cm
1800 m (1968 yd)	42 cm (16.5")

Horizontal Coriolis drift South

Mexico City is located at latitude 19.43, which is 2160 km north of the Equator. We will use this latitude as a comparison, to see how projectiles there are affected by Coriolis drift. Although it is not realistic that the atmospheric conditions such as air temperature, air pressure and humidity are identical to those at the 59th parallel north, these variables are ignored in the comparison in order to isolate the Coriolis effect. The drift in the tables below refer to drift to the right in the direction of shooting.

Table 45: 6.5x55

- 130 gn (8.42 grams) match bullet
- BC (G7): 0.274
- 900 m/s (2950 fps) muzzle velocity

Distance in m (yd)	Horizontal Coriolis drift in cm (inches)
500 m (546 yd)	0.8 cm (0.31")
600 m	1.2 cm
700 m (765 yd)	1.7 cm (0.66")
800 m	2.3 cm
900 m (984 yd)	3 cm (1.1")
1000 m	3.9 cm
1100 m (1202 yd)	4.9 cm (1.92")
1200 m	6.1 cm

Table 46: .338 Lapua Magnum

- 250 gn (16.2 grams) match bullet
- BC (G7): 0.322
- 905 m/s (2970 fps) muzzle velocity

Distance in m (yd)	Horizontal Coriolis drift in cm (inches)
800 m (874 yd)	2.1 cm (0.82")
900 m	2.8 cm
1000 m (1093 yd)	3.6 cm (1.4")
1100 m	4.5 cm
1200 m (1312 yd)	5.6 cm (2.2")
1300 m	6.9 cm
1400 m (1531 yd)	8.3 cm (3.2")
1500 m	10 cm
1600 m (1749 yd)	12 cm (4.7")
1700 m	13.9 cm
1800 m (1968 yd)	16.2 cm (6.3")

As shown in the tables above, there is a considerable difference in the Coriolis effect between northern and southern latitudes. The comparison with Mexico City shows that the Coriolis effect is negligible this far south at all but very long ranges, and even then, the drift is much less than in the north. The drift at the 19th parallel north is approximately 40% of the drift at the 59th parallel north.

There is one detail about the horizontal component of the Coriolis effect that is worth noting. The Coriolis effect does not increase proportionally with the length of the trajectory. The Coriolis force has a greater impact at longer distances because the projectile travels slower the further it flies. This means that the Coriolis effect has a proportionally greater impact the longer a bullet's trajectory is. In the above example from the 59th parallel north with a .338 Lapua

Magnum, the difference in drift between 1000 and 1100 meters is 1.5 cm, but the difference in drift between 1500 and 1600 meters is 4.8 cm. There are thus a couple of fundamental aspects of the Coriolis effect: firstly, it is practically insignificant below certain absolute distances, and secondly, we need to pay relatively more attention to the Coriolis effect the longer we shoot with a given caliber, since the Coriolis effect does not increase proportionally with the length of the bullet trajectory. The latter is, of course, not only true about the Coriolis drift, but also bullet drop, wind drift, and gyroscopic drift. The lower velocity of a projectile late in the trajectory causes significant external ballistic challenges.

Eötvös drift North

Note that all tables below labelled *eastward* assume a shot 90 degrees to the east. Conversely, the tables labelled *westward* assume a trajectory 270 degrees to the west. The Eötvös effect on trajectories that are not aimed directly to the east or west will be discussed further below, under the heading *Directional sensitivity of the Eötvös effect*.

Table 47: 6.5x55 eastward

- Latitude 59 (i.e. Alaska, central Canada or southern Sweden)
- 130 gn (8.42 grams) match bullet
- BC (G7): 0.274
- 900 m/s (2950 fps) muzzle velocity

Distance in m (yd)	Eötvös drift (less absolute bullet drop, higher point of impact) in cm (inches)
500 m ($\cong$550 yd)	+ 1.3 cm (0.5")
600 m	+ 2 cm
700 m	+ 3 cm
800 m ($\cong$875 yd)	+ 4 cm (1.6")
900 m	+ 5.3 cm
1000 m	+ 7 cm
1100 m	+ 9 cm
1200 m ($\cong$1300 yd)	+ 11 cm (4.3")

Table 48: 6.5x55 westward

The shot parameters are the same as in the previous table.

Distance in m (yd)	Eötvös drift (greater absolute bullet drop, lower point of impact) in cm (inches)
500 m ($\cong$550 yd)	- 1.3 cm (0.5")
600 m	- 2 cm
700 m	- 3 cm
800 m ($\cong$875 yd)	- 4 cm (1.6")
900 m	- 5.3 cm
1000 m	- 7 cm
1100 m	- 9 cm
1200 m ($\cong$1300 yd)	- 11 cm (4.3")

Table 49: 6.5 Creedmoor eastward

- Latitude 59
- 140 gn (9.07 grams) match bullet
- BC (G7): 0.304
- 820 m/s (2690 fps) muzzle velocity

Distance in m (yd)	Eötvös drift (less absolute bullet drop, higher point of impact) in cm (inches)
500 m (≅550 yd)	+ 1 cm (0.4")
600 m	+ 2 cm
700 m	+ 3 cm
800 m (≅875 yd)	+ 4 cm (1.6")
900 m	+ 6 cm
1000 m	+ 8 cm
1100 m	+ 10 cm (3.9")
1200 m (≅1300 yd)	+ 12 cm (4.7")

Table 50: 6.5 Creedmoor westward

The shot parameters are the same as in the previous table.

Distance in m (yd)	Eötvös drift (greater absolute bullet drop, lower point of impact) in cm (inches)
500 m (≅550 yd)	- 1 cm (0.4")
600 m	- 2 cm
700 m	- 3 cm
800 m (≅875 yd)	- 4 cm (1.6")
900 m	- 6 cm
1000 m	- 8 cm
1100 m	- 10 cm
1200 m (≅1300 yd)	- 12 cm (4.7")

Table 51: .308 Winchester eastward

- Latitude 59
- 168 gn (10.89 grams) match bullet
- BC (G7): 0.218
- 808 m/s (2650 fps) muzzle velocity

Distance in m (yd)	Eötvös drift (less absolute bullet drop, higher point of impact) in cm (inches)
500 m (≅550 yd)	+ 2 cm (0.8")
600 m	+ 3 cm
700 m	+ 4 cm
800 m (≅875 yd)	+ 5 cm (2")
900 m	+ 9 cm
1000 m	+ 12 cm
1100 m	+ 16 cm
1200 m (≅1300 yd)	+ 20 cm (8")

Table 52: .308 Winchester westward

The shot parameters are the same as in the previous table.

Distance in m (yd)	Eötvös drift (greater absolute bullet drop, lower point of impact) in cm (inches)
500 m (≅550 yd)	- 2 cm (0.8")
600 m	- 3 cm
700 m	- 4 cm
800 m (≅875 yd)	- 5 cm (2")
900 m	- 9 cm
1000 m	- 12 cm
1100 m	- 16 cm
1200 m (≅1300 yd)	- 20 cm (8")

Table 53: .338 Lapua Magnum eastward

- Latitude 59
- 250 gn (16.2 grams) match bullet
- BC (G7): 0.322
- 905 m/s (2970 fps) muzzle velocity

Distance in m (yd)	Eötvös drift (less absolute bullet drop, higher point of impact) in cm (inches)
800 m (≅875 yd)	+ 4 cm (1.6")
900 m	+ 5 cm
1000 m	+ 7 cm
1100 m	+ 9 cm
1200 m	+ 11 cm
1300 m (≅1420 yd)	+ 13 cm (5.1")
1400 m	+ 17 cm
1500 m	+ 20 cm
1600 m	+ 26 cm
1700 m	+ 29 cm
1800 m (≅1970 yd)	+ 35 cm (13.8")

Table 54: .338 Lapua Magnum westward

The shot parameters are the same as in the previous table.

Distance in m (yd)	Eötvös drift (greater absolute bullet drop, lower point of impact) in cm (inches)
800 m ($\cong$875 yd)	- 4 cm (1.6")
900 m	- 5 cm
1000 m	- 7 cm
1100 m	- 9 cm
1200 m	- 11 cm
1300 m ($\cong$1420 yd)	- 13 cm (5.1")
1400 m	- 17 cm
1500 m	- 20 cm
1600 m	- 26 cm
1700 m	- 29 cm
1800 m ($\cong$1970 yd)	- 35 cm (13.8")

Eötvös drift at the Equator

As mentioned above, the Eötvös effect is strongest at the Equator and weakest at the poles, in contrast to the horizontal component of the Coriolis effect. The tables below are calculated at the latitude of the Equator (0), where the Eötvös effect has the greatest impact. The parameters for projectiles and charges in the examples below are the same as in the examples above. All other parameters of the shot, other than latitude, are assumed to be the same, in order to isolate the Eötvös effect. Again, all tables labelled *eastward* assume a shot 90 degrees to the east. Conversely, the tables labelled *westward* assume a trajectory 270 degrees to the west.

Table 55: 6.5x55 eastward

- Latitude 0
- 130 gn (8.42 grams) match bullet
- BC (G7): 0.274
- 900 m/s (2950 fps) muzzle velocity

Distance in m (yd)	Eötvös drift (less absolute bullet drop, higher point of impact) in cm (inches)
500 m ($\cong$550 yd)	+ 2.6 cm (1")
600 m	+ 4 cm
700 m	+ 5.6 cm
800 m ($\cong$875 yd)	+ 8 cm (3.1")
900 m	+ 11 cm
1000 m	+ 14 cm
1100 m	+ 18 cm
1200 m ($\cong$1300 yd)	+ 23 cm (9")

Table 56: 6.5 Creedmoor eastward

- Latitude 0
- 140 gn (9.07 grams) match bullet
- BC (G7): 0.304
- 820 m/s (2690 fps) muzzle velocity

Distance in m (yd)	Eötvös drift (less absolute bullet drop, higher point of impact) in cm (inches)
500 m (≅550 yd)	+3 cm (1.2")
600 m	+4 cm
700 m	+6 cm
800 m (≅875 yd)	+8 cm (3.1")
900 m	+11 cm
1000 m	+15 cm
1100 m	+19 cm
1200 m (≅1300 yd)	+24 cm (9.4")

Table 57: .308 Winchester eastward

- Latitude 0
- 168 gn (10.89 grams) match bullet
- BC (G7): 0.218
- 808 m/s (2650 fps) muzzle velocity

Distance in m (yd)	Eötvös drift (less absolute bullet drop, higher point of impact) in cm (inches)
500 m (≅550 yd)	+ 4 cm (1.6")
600 m	+ 5.5 cm
700 m	+ 8 cm
800 m (≅875 yd)	+ 11.6 cm (4.6")
900 m	+ 16 cm
1000 m	+ 22 cm
1100 m	+ 29 cm
1200 m (≅1300 yd)	+ 38 cm (14.9")

As seen from the examples above, the impact of the Eötvös effect on the bullet trajectory is approximately twice as large at the Equator as compared to at the 59th parallel north. The amount of drift at shots straight to the east or west is identical, but affects the trajectory in the opposite way. If we get a point of impact that is 4 inches high when shooting to the east, and then turn around and shoot west in the exact opposite direction, we will have a point of impact that is 4 inches low instead.

Directional sensitivity of the Eötvös effect

The Eötvös effect is directionally sensitive, unlike the horizontal component of the Coriolis effect. The impact of the Eötvös effect on the projectile trajectory depends on the direction in which the shot is fired, as illustrated in the tables below. Note that all tables below illustrating the directional sensitivity of the Eötvös effect assumes shooting at the latitude of the equator. All parameters of the shot, other than azimuth, are the same as in the tables above.

Table 58: 6.5 Creedmoor 45 degrees eastward

Distance in m (yd)	Eötvös drift (less absolute bullet drop, higher point of impact) in cm (inches)
500 m (≅550 yd)	+ 2 cm (0.8")
600 m	+ 3 cm
700 m	+ 4 cm
800 m (≅875 yd)	+ 6 cm (2.4")
900 m	+ 8 cm
1000 m	+ 10 cm
1100 m	+ 14 cm
1200 m (≅1300 yd)	+ 17 cm (6.7")

Table 59: 6.5 Creedmoor 90 degrees eastward

Distance in m (yd)	Eötvös drift (less absolute bullet drop, higher point of impact)
500 m (≅550 yd)	+ 3 cm (1.2")
600 m	+ 4 cm
700 m	+ 6 cm
800 m (≅875 yd)	+ 8 cm (3.1")
900 m	+ 11 cm
1000 m	+ 15 cm
1100 m	+ 19 cm
1200 m (≅1300 yd)	+ 24 cm (9.4")

Table 60: 6.5 Creedmoor 225 degrees westward

Distance in m (yd)	Eötvös drift (greater absolute bullet drop, lower point of impact)
500 m (≅550 yd)	- 2 cm (0.8"
600 m	- 3 cm
700 m	- 4 cm
800 m (≅875 yd)	- 6 cm (2.4")
900 m	- 8 cm
1000 m	- 10 cm
1100 m	- 13 cm
1200 m (≅1300 yd)	- 17 cm (6.7")

Causes of the Coriolis effect

It is quite complicated to grasp the physical consequences of living on a giant rotating sphere. On reflection, it seems like a rather strange place to live. Unfortunately, we have no choice in this regard. This section discusses the causes of the Coriolis force in more detail. It is of course not necessary to understand in order to be able to compensate for the effects, but it may be interesting for the curious.

The horizontal component

The Coriolis force is normally explained as a combination of two dynamical principles, both caused by the rotating Earth: differences in absolute velocity and conservation of angular momentum.[19] We will start by discussing differences in absolute velocities, and then

---

[19] Persson (1998), Herrera and Morett (2016)

the conservation of angular momentum. For example, a point at the latitude of Stockholm, capital city of Sweden, is rotating around the Earth's axis at a speed of about 800 km/h (approximately 500 mph), which is about half the speed of that at the Equator (1670 km/h or 1037 mph). A point in the north of Sweden, at the 67th parallel north, is instead rotating at about 620 km/h (approximately 385 mph). The differences in absolute rotational speed are due to the varying diameter of the Earth. Since the Earth has a larger diameter at the Equator, a point closer to the Equator rotates faster than a point further away from the Equator.

When we fire a projectile in any direction, we only affect the linear motion of the projectile, i.e. we accelerate the projectile forward. However, we do not affect the tangential velocity of the projectile, i.e. the velocity that the projectile already has due to the rotation of the Earth. This lateral movement of the projectile continues at the same velocity as it had before it was fired.

When shooting at very long distances, the difference in lateral velocity between the projectile and the target begins to affect the point of impact of a projectile. When we shoot north in the northern hemisphere, and the distance is great enough, the bullet hits to the right of the target because it carries a higher tangential velocity than the target, and therefore seems to drift to the right. When we shoot southward in the northern hemisphere, the bullet also impacts to the right of the target, because the bullet has a lower tangential velocity than the target, and again seems to drift to the right. It is important to understand, however, that the *Coriolis drift is present regardless of which direction we shoot.*

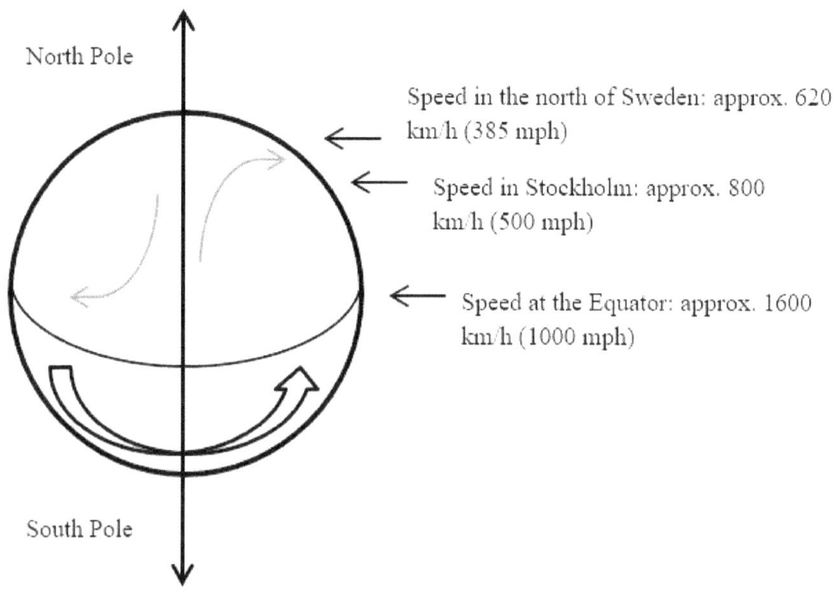

The red lines in Figure 17 represent projectiles being fired. The projectile fired north moves to the right of the target because it carries a higher tangential velocity than its target. Conversely, the projectile fired south carries a lower lateral velocity than its target. Both of these cases result in the projectile impacting to right if not compensated for. Exactly the reverse occurs in the southern hemisphere, so that all shots appear to move to the left, although they simply retain the tangential velocity they had when they were fired.

In the figure above, I only included shots fired in the north-south direction. Let's observe an example of what happens when shooting eastward or westward in the northern hemisphere, to illustrate that the Coriolis force acts in any direction.

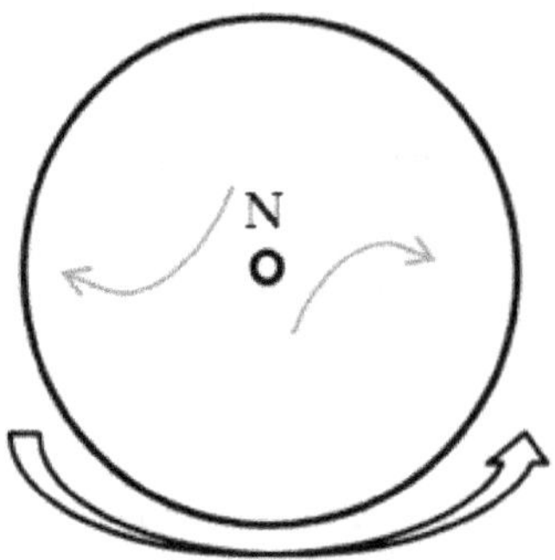

Figure 18 above shows the Earth from above the North Pole. The red lines represent bullet trajectories. Of course, none of these illustrations are to scale. They are visual exaggerations, drawn to help understand the dynamic principles of the Coriolis effect. In the image above, the Earth is rotating to the east around the North Pole. The red arrows represent bullet trajectories, which appear to deviate from their trajectory towards the target due to the Earth's rotation. It only makes sense for the arrows in the image above to veer off to the right when we imagine that we are rotating with the Earth as we look down on it. Instead, if we imagine that we are looking down at the Earth but not rotating counterclockwise with it, it would be better to draw the arrows in a straight path, since the projectiles are not actually veering off. It is the reference frame (the Earth) that moves in relation to them, giving the impression that the projectiles are deviating from a straight path. The same effect occurs on the southern hemisphere, of course, only then the projectiles appear to drift to the left rather than to the right.

For a long time, only differences in absolute velocity were used to explain the Coriolis effect. It is now considered that differences in absolute velocity account for about half of the Coriolis effect, and that the other half of the force depends on the conservation of angular momentum.

Angular momentum basically means the kinetic energy of bodies moving in a circular path, as opposed to bodies moving in a straight path. The explanation is that projectiles that rotate at a certain velocity with the Earth's rotation rate and at the same time move in a north-south direction attempt to preserve their angular momentum. Since the circumference of the Earth becomes larger or smaller when the projectile travels over it, in order for the angular momentum to be conserved the tangential velocity of the projectile must increase or decrease.

For instance, when a projectile is fired from south to north in the northern hemisphere, the radius of the circle that the projectile travels in around Earth becomes smaller. In order for the angular momentum to be conserved, the tangential velocity of the projectile must increase, reinforcing the Coriolis effect. When a projectile is fired from the north to south in the northern hemisphere, the radius of the circle in which the projectile travels around the Earth's axis increases. In order for the angular momentum to be conserved, the tangential velocity of the projectile must decrease, in turn reinforcing the Coriolis effect.

There is one fact about the physical shape of the Earth that enhances the Coriolis effect: the Earth is not round. The Earth is roughly what is called an *ellipsoid*, which means it is slightly oval. The Earth's circumference has increased around the Equator, because the centrifugal force is strongest there, while the two poles appear slightly flattened. In a technical sense, the Earth is not an ellipsoid; due to its varying topography it is too uneven to be a true ellipsoid, but for simplicity's sake we can liken it to an ellipsoid. As a result, differences in the rotational speed at different latitudes on Earth are amplified compared to a perfect globe. So, the ellipsoidal shape of the Earth has increased the rotational speed differences between different latitudes, thus amplifying the Coriolis effect.

Below is the formula to calculate the horizontal Coriolis drift of a ballistic trajectory:

$$Coriolis\ drift = 0{,}000072 \times D \times \sin(Lat) \times tof$$

0.000072 = Earth's rotation speed in rad/second.

D = distance to the target in meters.

Sin(Lat) = Sine of the latitude from which the shot is made.

tof = Time of flight, i.e. the flight time of the projectile.

The obtained solution is in hundredths of a meter, i.e. centimeters, and looks like this: 0.0XXXXX.

Causes of the Eötvös effect

The Eötvös effect, which is often lumped together with the Coriolis effect, is also due to the rotation of the Earth, but affects the bullet in the vertical plane. The Eötvös effect is usually defined as a change in perceived gravity due to a change in centrifugal acceleration. In simpler terms, the Eötvös effect is a result of the tug of war between Earth's gravity and the centrifugal force created by Earth's rotation. When shooting east, in the direction of Earth's rotation, the bullet exceeds the speed of Earth's rotation, causing the centrifugal acceleration to overcome the gravitational force and the bullet to rise in its trajectory. The result is that the bullet impacts higher on the target. A shot in a westerly direction has the opposite effect, as the bullet travels slower than the Earth's rotational speed. Therefore, the centrifugal acceleration is weakened and the force of gravity relatively stronger, resulting in a lower impact on the target.

While the physical causes of the Eötvös effect are probably easier to grasp than the horizontal component of the Coriolis effect, it is more difficult to compensate for. This is because to compensate for it, one must take into account not only latitude but also direction (azimuth). The centrifugal acceleration increases or decreases more or less in relation to gravity depending on the direction in which we shoot. If we shoot straight east or west, it has the greatest impact, but it has a lesser impact if we shoot for example 45 degrees east or west. In this way, the Eötvös effect is *directionally sensitive in* a way that the horizontal component of the Coriolis effect is not. If we shoot straight north or south, the Eötvös effect does not affect the bullet trajectory at all, because we do not affect the velocity of the bullet in relation to Earth's rotational speed.

The following is one way to calculate the Eötvös drift of a projectile. The formula does not give an answer in a unit of measure, but rather a correction factor that is multiplied by the absolute drop of the projectile at a given distance to give the true drop.

$$F_c = 1 - \frac{2 \times 0.00007292 \times V_0}{9.806} \, \text{cosine}(Lat) \, \text{sine}(A)$$

In which:

F_c = correction factor by which data for projectile drop at a certain distance are multiplied to obtain the correct drop.

0.00007292 = Earth's rotational speed (0.00007292 Rad per second).

V_0 = muzzle velocity of the projectile.

9.806 = standard measure of gravity.

Lat = latitude from which the shot is made.

A = the direction of the shot in degrees (Azimuth), counted clockwise from the North Pole. See figure below for reference.

Figure 19: compass rose for angles

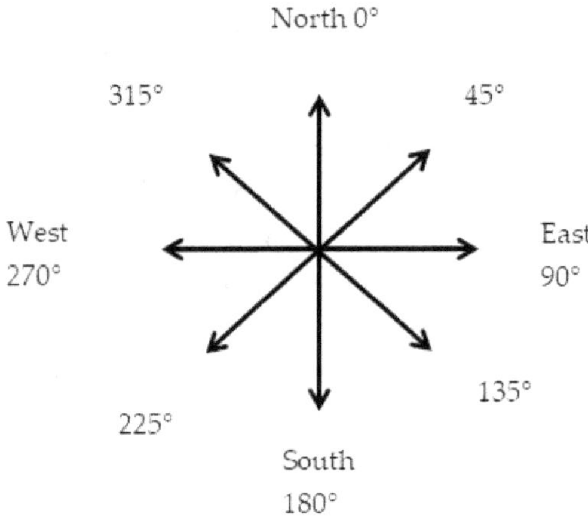

One thing to keep in mind when measuring the angle to compensate for the Eötvös effect is that we want to measure from the geographical North Pole, not the magnetic north pole. This is because the two are not in exactly the same place, and using the magnetic north pole introduces an error in the calculation.

SHOOTING UPWARD OR DOWNWARD

When shooting rifles at upward or downward angles and compensating for distance (gravity), only the horizontal distance to the target needs to be considered, and not the diagonal (line of sight) distance. The diagonal line of sight to a target is always longer than the horizontal, but it is the horizontal distance that should to be compensated for. This is counter-intuitive, because we are used to measuring the distance to the target and adjusting accordingly. Since the diagonal line of sight to the target is longer than the horizontal distance to the target when shooting up or down, we will overcompensate for the distance if we don't perform the calculation correctly.

Figure 20: angular distance

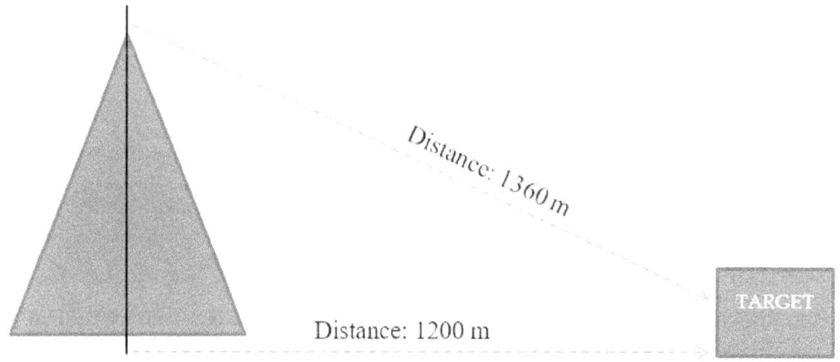

The lower dashed line in Figure 20 above represents the horizontal (ground) distance to the target 1200 meters ($\cong$1300 yd) away. The upper dashed line represents the distance to the target on a 30-degree angle to the same target. Due to the elevation, the diagonal distance to the target from the shooting site is 1360 meters ($\cong$1490 yd). Gravity pulls the projectile downward as much when shooting at a 30-degree angle as when shooting along the ground, even though the diagonal distance to the target is longer. Thus, gravity acts only over the horizontal distance of the projectile, and it does not matter how the absolute length of the projectile's trajectory is affected by the inclination. This means that if we compensate to shoot 1360 meters instead of 1200, we will probably shoot over the target, depending on how big the target is. In order to compensate correctly, we need to compensate for the distance to the target at ground level, i.e. the horizontal distance, and not the diagonal distance.

The relation between the horizontal distance and the diagonal distance is always the same at a certain angle, and can be easily accounted for, given that we can approximate the shooting angle. If we assume that we shoot at an angle of 30%, for instance, the horizontal distance will always be 13.5% shorter than the diagonal distance. The *relative difference* is therefore constant when shooting at a 30-degree angle. However, the *absolute difference* obviously differs depending on the distance at which we shoot. In the example above, the difference is 160 meters because the horizontal distance is 1200 meters. If we instead assume a horizontal distance of 600 meters and the same angle, the error will be half as large, that is, 80 meters. 80 meters is still a significant measurement error in, for example, competitive shooting, and depending on the target and caliber it is certainly possible to miss the target because of it.

So how do we solve the problem of the difference between the diagonal and horizontal distances? As with everything in external ballistics, there is a formula for this. It's quite straightforward, and it requires borrowing from trigonometry because what we're discussing is basically large triangles. When shooting from a height, or vice versa up toward a height, we hopefully know the distance from the shooting location to the target. We can measure this either by eye, rangefinder or by angular measurement in our rifle sight. This is the *absolute distance* to the target, but it is not what we have to adjust for when shooting at an angle. We need a way to find the *horizontal distance* in order to adjust the sight correctly.

The formula is as follows:

$$D_h = D_d \times cosine\ of\ the\ angle$$

Where D_h = horizontal distance

D_d = diagonal (measured) distance

Cosine is a trigonometric function that can be used to find the distance in the ground plane from the diagonal distance. We can of course calculate the cosine for each occasion, but the easiest way is to have a table of cosines for angles that we can use quickly when we need it. An example of such a table is below.

Table 61: Cosine of angle

Angle (degrees)	Cosine
5	0.99
10	0.98
15	0.96
20	0.93
25	0.90
30	0.86
35	0.81
40	0.76
45	0.70
50	0.64
55	0.57
60	0.5
65	0.42
70	0.34

Let's look at the same example we had earlier and try to calculate the horizontal distance. Suppose that we are on a hill and we are going to shoot at a target on the ground. We measure the distance to the target as 820 meters, and we estimate or measure that the angle of the shot is about 25 degrees. Table 61 above shows that the cosine of 25 degrees is 0.9. When we then multiply our diagonal distance by the cosine of 30 degrees, we get 820 x 0.9 = 728 meters. It does not matter if the shot is at an upward or downward angle, the solution looks the same. It also doesn't matter if we make the calculation in meters, yards, inches or any other measurement; the formula works the same as long as the same unit of length is used consistently.

We can make our own table that already contains some common distances and common angles, so we don't have to do any calculations at all when it's time to shoot. Some competitions do not allow electronic aids such as mobile phone or calculators, and in that case, we need to have good tables from the start.

Assessment of angles

Now we know how to compensate for shooting at angles upward or downward, but how do we know what angle we're shooting at? The first thing to know is that most people *overestimate* angles in nature. Most hills we see out in nature do not result in more than 10-20 degrees of shooting angle. 30 degrees also occurs but is often the largest angle we see, except in mountainous terrain. 45 degrees is unusual and only occurs where the surface is relatively hard, and better resists the tendency of gravity to pull everything downward, such as a mountain or a cliff. We can, of course, find more extreme angles in nature, but these are usually mountains, such as when shooting off the edge of a cliff.

There is a concept called the *angle of repose*, or *friction angle*. The angle of repose describes the angle at which a fine-grained material, such as sand or soil, settles in a pile in relation to the ground. Soil, which is the most common substrate in nature, has an angle of repose of 30-45 degrees, and can vary quite a lot depending on the exact composition of the soil and the mutual friction between the grains. Of course, in nature, the soil has not just fallen in a new fresh pile from the sky, but has been pulled down and stomped on by animals and nature for ages, resulting in an angle that is usually much less than 30 degrees.

There are also mechanical and electronic aids to help us assess angles. Modern laser rangefinders also often measure the angle to the target. There are also mechanical gauges that can be mounted around the tube of a rifle scope, and when we angle the weapon up or down, a small drum with a scale on it rotates and we can read the angle. Sometimes such aids are allowed in competition, and sometimes not.

THE TRANSONIC TRANSITION

The transonic transition is the period at the end of a projectile's trajectory, when it transitions from supersonic velocity to subsonic. The transonic transition starts already at Mach 1.2, when the bullet can have a velocity of over 400 meters per second (900 mph), which is well above the speed of sound in most cases. But even though the bullet is supersonic, the dynamic instability caused by the airflow around it can steer it off course. This is important to understand, because otherwise the accuracy of a projectile at the end of its trajectory may be overestimated.

When a projectile loses velocity at the end of its trajectory, it enters the transonic phase at about 1.2 times the speed of sound, which at 20° C (68 degrees F) is about 411 m/s (1348 mph). The transonic phase is generally said to be around Mach 0.8 - Mach 1.2, and a bullet that is well stabilized can in theory continue to fly and hit its target at subsonic velocities, but in general we want to avoid the bullet slowing down to subsonic speeds because it tends to get destabilized in the transonic phase. While the bullet may stabilize again after the transition to subsonic speed, it may also have come out of its intended trajectory during the transition, so that it no longer hits the target, or at least not where the shooter intended to hit.

The deterioration of projectile stability in the transonic transition is due to the fact that the center of pressure is shifted forward on the projectile as it loses velocity, and the overturning force is strengthened. This changes the angle of attack of the projectile, which affects the trajectory of the bullet. The main factor that influences the speed of sound is air temperature: the colder the temperature, the lower the speed of sound. Below is a table showing how the speed of sound changes with temperature in dry air.

Table 62: The speed of sound

Temperature in Celsius (Fahrenheit)	Speed of sound in meters per second (mph)
-30° C (-22° F)	312 m/s (698 mph)
-20° C (-4° F)	318 m/s (711 mph)
-10° C (14° F)	325 m/s (727 mph)
0° C (32° F)	331 m/s (740 mph)
10° C (50° F)	337 m/s (754 mph)
20° C (68° F)	343 m/s (767 mph)
30° C (86° F)	349 m/s (781 mph)

As can be observed in Table 62, the variance of the speed of sound at different temperatures is significant. This means that the transonic transition occurs at different parts of a projectile's trajectory depending on the air temperature. The transonic transition occurs earlier in the trajectory in warmer temperatures, and later in colder temperatures. At Mach 1.2, which is considered the upper limit of the transonic transition, occurs at 30° C at about 420 m/s, and at -20° C at about 380 m/s.

Figure 21: higher supersonic projectile

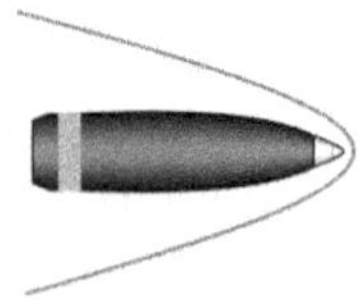

Figure 21 shows a bullet at supersonic speed. The blue line represents the wavefront of air that is compressed and pushed away by the bullet as it passes. The wavefront spreads outwards from the bullet and is perceived by our ears as a bang as the bullet passes. The angle of the wavefront is called the *Mach angle*, and it can be used to calculate relatively accurately how fast a projectile is traveling. When the wavefront angle is smaller, the projectile travels faster and vice versa.

Figure 22: lower supersonic projectile

The bullet in Figure 22 above is also supersonic, but is traveling much slower and is approaching the end of its flight at supersonic speed. It is close to the transonic transition. The Mach angle is much flatter now, indicating the slower speed.

Figure 23: transonic transition

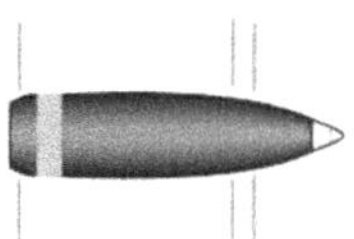

The bullet in Figure 23 above is in the transonic transition. The bullet itself is subsonic, but at certain points on the bullet the air is accelerated and becomes supersonic. The supersonic waves caused by the bullet are shown in the image above as blue lines. The air around the bullet has gone from being pushed around the bullet in a continuous wave front to being accelerated to supersonic speed at certain areas of the bullet.

Depending on the purpose of the shooting situation, there are of course reasons other than accuracy to avoid the transonic transition. In hunting, it is often inappropriate to hit game with subsonic bullets because the bullet's expansion mechanism does not work well at such low velocities. In addition, the impact energy will be lower than the minimum recommended for many game species.

SHOOTING AT MOVING TARGETS

Shooting at moving targets differs in two fundamental ways from shooting at stationary targets:

1. Since the target is moving, the shooter typically also needs to move. A (partial) exception is the more stationary ambush method, which will be explained below.

2. The target continues to move after the bullet has left the barrel, which means that the movement of the target must be taken into account in the ballistic solution. This means that we have to shoot in front of the target to hit it. The only exception to this would be if a strong crosswind causes drift in the direction that the target is moving, thus compensating for the movement.

There are three basic methods of shooting at moving targets, although these overlap to some extent. These methods will be explained in more detail below. The three methods are:

- **Swing-through**
- **Ambush**
- **Sustained lead**

A fundamental principle of shooting moving targets with a rifle scope is to use as low a magnification (power) as possible. The lower the magnification, the larger the field of view, and the earlier the shooter can detect the target. A higher magnification reduces the field of view, and the shooter can easily be surprised by the target as it passes into the field of view. It is also more likely that if the shooter is inattentive for a moment, he or she will miss the window of opportunity to shoot the target. It is also important to have the correct parallax setting on the scope, because when following the target, we do not always look straight through the scope, and therefore risk parallax error at the moment of shooting. Correct parallax adjustment is of course always important, but is even more important when shooting moving targets at longer distances because the eye may not be perfectly aligned with the center axis of the rifle scope.

Swing through

Everyone who shoots clay pigeons is familiar with the swing-through method. It involves starting to aim behind the moving target, and then sweeping the weapon forward through the target in a swinging motion, firing immediately upon reaching the desired point of aim in front of the target. The method is intuitive and works well for standing shooting at close targets, such as clay targets or duck hunting.

Ambush

The ambush method means aiming at a point where the target is expected to pass, and firing directly when the target appears at the point of aim. This is the most static of the methods. However, the shooter usually has to be mobile in his shooting position to observe the target or find it in his scope, which means that it is not a completely static method. When aiming and firing, however, the shooting position is static, unlike the other methods. In the event that the shooter wants to fire again at a target that has passed by, he has to redirect the weapon to a new point where the target is expected to pass. Ambush is a suitable method when it is known where the target will pass, such as through channeling terrain, or if there is only a small window of time in which to fire at the target, such as a doorway or forest clearing.

Sustained lead

Sustained lead (also known as tracking) means keeping a constant lead[20] on the target, and firing when the shooter is satisfied with the point of aim. The shooter adjusts his shooting position so that he can follow the target. Sustained lead is similar to the swing through method but does not have to start behind the target, nor does the shooter fire immediately when the lead is correct, but can follow the target and fine-tune the point of aim before firing. Sustained lead is suitable when there are no obstacles between the shooter and the target, so that the target can be spotted and followed some distance before firing. Sustained lead is also often a better method of dealing with the potential sources of error discussed in the sections below.

Ambush and sustained lead are the methods most commonly used in long-range precision shooting. Different shooters usually have a preference for one or the other method, but it is important to understand that they are also differently suited to different shooting situations, as noted above. In my experience, the sustained lead method is excellent for most applications except for those where the target is only visible for a short time, in which case the ambush method is more suitable.

---

[20] A constant point of aim in front of the target.

Shooting position

Shooting standing against moving targets at very short distances is easier than lying down, because it is easier to move our body from side to side standing than lying down. By the same logic, seated shooting at moving targets is easier than prone, especially if we have a stable support for the weapon. The prone shooting position is the most stable position, as the body has the most contact with the ground, which in turn means that it is more difficult to change direction of aim when lying down. A common feature of the various shooting positions when shooting at moving targets is that there is a limited time window for shooting, i.e. a limited time when we can fire the weapon in one position before we have to move our entire body to redirect the rifle toward the target. We cannot follow a moving target indefinitely without the shooting position becoming untenable, and we have to change our physical position and direction completely. In the standing shooting position, this time window is longer because we can turn our legs and hips to follow a target. In the prone position the time window is much shorter, because of the more rigid shooting position. In practice, we start the movement and aim roughly at the target in a less comfortable shooting position, and then fine-tune the point of aim and fire when we get into the right position, i.e. a more comfortable position. In the ambush method, on the other hand, the shooter does not have to follow the target in the rifle scope, but can focus on firing at the right moment.

Lead

All of the methods described above mean that we need to aim in front of the moving target. This is called *lead*. Lead is necessary because the bullet does not hit the target immediately after firing, but it takes a certain amount of time for the bullet to reach the target (time of flight). During this time, a moving target moves a certain distance. This means that faster moving targets, and moving targets at longer distances require more lead than slower targets and targets at shorter distances.

Calculating lead

In competitive shooting, it is best to be well prepared with ballistic tables for the situations we may find ourselves in during competition. Such ballistic tables may also include adjustments for shooting at moving targets at different distances and speeds. There are, of course, excellent ballistic calculators that can be used to calculate lead, but we may not have the time to do this during a competition, and we may not be able to rely on technology to do so. It is also quite simple to calculate lead using the formula presented below.

Mathematically, the calculation of lead involves the variables 1. speed of the target and 2. time of flight of the projectile to the target. There are two different approaches to assessing target speed: either assuming it, or measuring it with a rifle scope or spotting scope. Assuming the target's speed is the same as applying knowledge of how fast such a target usually moves. For example, the average walking speed of a human is 5 km/h, and a moose trots at around 20 km/h. Such knowledge can be used to calculate how much lead is needed to hit the target at a certain distance, but it is mostly suitable when the target is moving at a right angle from the bullet's path. Be aware that when we use prior knowledge of the target's speed, we must consider the angle of the target's movement from the bullet path, i.e. when the target is not moving at an angle of 90 degrees from the bullet path. This is done by multiplying the speed of movement by the sine of the angle of movement of the target from the line of sight. This can of course be done beforehand in tabular form, but since it is not difficult to measure the target's speed of movement in the moment, this is often the more convenient method.

The preferred, and more precise, way to estimate the speed of movement of a target is to measure it ourselves, either using a rifle scope or a spotting scope. In this case, the scope needs to be equipped with a grid system for angular measurement, such as Milliradian (MRAD) or Minute of Angle (MOA). The longer the time we measure the movement of the target, the more accurate the measurement will be. Measuring the speed of the target is usually the best way, because we don't have to take account of the angle of movement of the target.

The estimation is made by measuring the time it takes the target to travel between two points in the rifle scope (or spotting scope), usually 10 or 20 MRAD (at 500 meters 5 and 10 meters respectively). When measuring the speed of the target, it is important to use a low magnification setting to increase the field of view. There is no need to include kilometers per hour or meters per second in the calculation of target speed; this will only complicate things. It is easiest to simply measure the target's speed of movement in milliradians per second (or MOA if that is what we have) and to compensate in milliradians (MOA). This way, no conversion between different units of measurement is required.

The formula for calculating lead is:

$$lead\ (MRAD) = target\ speed\ x\ tof$$

In which:

target speed = number of MRAD or MOA the target moves per second

tof = time of flight of the projectile to the target at the current distance

It doesn't matter if we use MRAD or MOA in the calculation. As long as we use one angular measure consistently in the formula, it works. Let's say we are shooting at a moving target at 1000 meters, and we measure the target's speed to 10 MRAD (10 meters) in 7 seconds. Thus, the target moves at 10/7 = 1.4 MRAD per second. The flight time of the projectile in my competition rifle in 6.5x55 mm to 1000 meters is 1.73 seconds. 1.4 MRAD/second x 1.73 seconds = 2.422 MRAD. Thus, the lead to the target at that speed, at 1000 meters, is 2.4 MRAD. It is obviously not practical to make such a calculation on the spot behind the scope, but it certainly can be done, especially when the shooter has a good understanding of projectile flight time at different distances. When hunting, the game can move erratically and at varying speeds, which significantly complicates the situation. Shooting at moving targets at long distances is the most difficult form of rifle shooting.

Conflicting variables

It should be noted that all the different adjustments made when compensating for external ballistic phenomena can counteract each other, and must therefore be harmonized in any ballistic solution. The most common example is gyroscopic drift and wind drift. When the wind is blowing from the right in the shooting direction, and we are shooting at longer distances, the gyroscopic drift partially compensates for wind drift, and reduces the need for wind drift compensation. On the other hand, when the wind blows from the left in the direction of fire, wind drift and gyroscopic drift must be both compensated for, and can thus be added together. Similarly, when shooting at a moving target, wind drift must be taken into account and may result in the need to increase or decrease the lead. Typically, ballistic calculators do this for us automatically, and it is not something that we need to do ourselves. But when we are shooting without a ballistic calculator, we need to be mindful of this. Curiously, if we do not compensate our rifle scope for wind, but "hold off" using the crosshairs, it may be necessary to aim behind a moving target, provided the wind is strong enough to cause the bullet to "catch up" with the moving target and hit it.

Reaction time and other aspects

Since the target is in motion, any time delay in shooting can cause a miss. Reaction time is the time from when the shooter decides to pull the trigger to when the trigger is pulled. It is vital to keep the rifle sight at the correct lead while the rifle is being fired. Every shooter has a slightly different reaction time, but all shooters have a reaction time to consider. It is quite common for shooters to miss a moving target, because their aiming movement stops when they decide to fire the rifle. It is of great importance that the shooter focuses on maintaining the lead when squeezing the trigger. Ideally, as is true in general about precision shooting, the shooter should be surprised by the shot. This is an indication that the shooter is focused entirely on sight picture, and not anticipating the shot.

Lock time is the time that passes between squeezing the trigger and the firing pin igniting the primer, igniting the powder charge in the cartridge.

Dwell time is the time between when the primer ignites the powder charge and when the bullet leaves the muzzle of the rifle.

The delaying aspects discussed above are all extremely short periods of time, but they add up to a long enough delay to miss what we are aiming at. The faster the target moves and the longer the distance, the more disciplined we have to be about keeping the target at the right point in the sight when we squeeze the trigger, as well as after squeezing the trigger.

Shooting from a moving platform

Rifle shooting from a moving platform is an interesting phenomenon, but not one that I have any personal experience with. In some countries people hunt from cars or helicopters, for example, and military forces obviously need to be able to engage targets from moving platforms such as armored vehicles and helicopters. In theory, shooting from a moving platform is the same as shooting at a moving target, but just the opposite. When a projectile is fired from a moving platform at an angle towards a target, it maintains its lateral velocity after leaving the barrel. Suppose a shooter is hunting deer from a helicopter. The deer is stationary while the helicopter is moving at 70 km/h at a right angle from the deer, and the distance to the deer is 200 meters. At that distance it takes approximately a quarter second for the bullet to reach the target, and at that distance the projectile has time to travel about 5 meters sideways. Thus, if the shooter does not compensate for his own speed, he will probably miss the target, even at a distance of 100 meters.

PRACTICAL APPLICATION

The above chapters of the book have aimed to give the reader an understanding of the various external ballistic factors. Once at the range or at a competition, it is time to apply this understanding in practice. The principle for doing this is straightforward: we solve the external ballistic problems one by one in order of magnitude, with the largest problem first. By solving the problems starting with the biggest problem first, we arrive at a ballistic solution which in the best case leads to hitting the target. If time is insufficient for solving what is in most cases minor ballistic considerations, like humidity or Coriolis drift, we can still rest assured that we have solved the major obstacles and will be roughly on target. The following is a check list for how a shooter should go about solving external ballistic problems. Note, however, that the list is somewhat of a simplification. Sometimes there is no wind at all, and it is quite rare to shoot in a significant angle. However, since these two factors have a potentially large impact on projectile trajectory, they must be considered.

1. Distance to the target and angle of fire

The primary problem to be solved, if it is not already known, is the distance to the target. If we don't know this distance, we are likely to miss our target, unless it is very close. The angle of the shot is included as an aspect of the distance to the target, because the angle needs to be taken into account when compensating for distance. However, as noted earlier in the book, shot angles over 30 degrees are rare, and most shot angles in practice are no greater than 20 degrees. Shooting in mountain environments is often more demanding and can entail steeper angles.

2. Wind drift

It is not always windy, but we must always consider wind, because the potential impact on the trajectory is significant. Solving ballistic problems 1 (distance) and 2 (wind drift) is in most shooting situations quite sufficient to hit what we are aiming at, given that the target is either stationary game or a competition target. What follows are factors of lesser importance, but may determine miss or hit at long distances for a given caliber, such as competition shooting or hunting at longer distances.

3. Gyroscopic drift

Gyroscopic drift should be taken into account when shooting common rifle calibers (i.e., 308 W, 6.5 mm or 7 mm caliber) at distances exceeding 600 meters, especially for bullets with lower ballistic coefficients (e.g. .308 Winchester). For higher ballistic coefficient match bullets, a significant effect of gyroscopic drift will occur at longer distances, such as 800 meters for 6.5x55 or 6.5 Creedmoor competition bullets.

Solving the problems of distance, wind and gyroscopic drift is usually sufficient, depending on the size of the target, to hit targets in long range rifle shooting, up to and above 1000 meters ($\cong 1100$ yd). Differences in air temperature can have a significant effect on the projectile trajectory, but this requires shooting at very long distances for a given caliber and that the temperature has changed several tens of degrees from the zeroing temperature, which must be considered unusual. Air temperature will often have a more significant internal ballistic effect on burn rate of the powder charge, rather than externally ballistic. Humidity, as we have seen in previous chapters, has so little effect that this variable can usually be ignored completely. However, it is worth bearing in mind that a bullet in heavy rain can cause the projectile to change course and miss the target. When shooting at very long ranges, and especially closer to the North or South Pole, the horizontal component of the Coriolis effect must also be taken into account. At very long ranges the Eötvös effect also must be considered, and especially when shooting closer to the equator.

One thing to note is that when shooting at long ranges, is it typically more likely that systematic shooting errors on the shooter's part will be more of a problem than for example temperature or humidity. A stable shooting position, a consistent cheek weld and keeping the crosshairs firmly on the target when squeezing the trigger are often more important than considering every minute detail of exterior ballistics. If the fundamentals of good shooting technique are not present, they must be firmly established before it is useful to consider minor exterior ballistic aspects.

Testing

No ballistic calculator is perfect, nor is the person who enters the parameters into the calculator. Neither is the company that manufactured the ammunition or the engineers responsible for measuring the ballistic coefficient of the bullets. The ballistic solutions provided by ballistic calculators are often excellent at short and medium distances, but sometimes discrepancies between reality and the calculator's solution can be seen at long and very long ranges. There is unfortunately no better solution than to go out and test our ballistic solutions on the shooting range to find out if they are correct or not. This is best done by test firing at different distances and checking how well our ballistic solutions match reality. When we do this, we usually find that the tables need some adjustment, especially at longer distances. This can be due to a number of variables, but the most common are incorrect muzzle velocity data and incorrect ballistic coefficient data. When shooting factory-loaded ammunition, we must be prepared for significant deviations in muzzle velocity between cartridges in the same batch, which obviously has a negative impact on the results.

DIVERGENCE TO INTERNAL BALLISTICS

There are aspects of internal ballistics that are so important to shooting, and specifically long-range shooting, that they ought to be mentioned in a book on external ballistics. This is because they have such a strong impact on the external ballistic potential of a round, that they need to be considered for the best results. The first is the need to know the exact muzzle velocity of the projectiles, in order to correctly model the trajectory. It is not enough to read on the box of factory-loaded ammunition to know what velocity it will have, as the muzzle velocity of a projectile depends on the length of the barrel, and therefore the time the bullet is propelled by the powder gases. Longer barrels typically give a higher velocity, provided the powder charge is the same. Often manufacturers have tested their ammunition in a test barrel that is longer than an average barrel for that caliber, which means that the velocity indicated on the box is higher than what we will get in our own rifle. This is a convenient way for the manufacturer to be able to print a higher number on the box, but not very helpful to shooters and hunters who want to know how fast their bullets are. Fortunately for us, the price of chronographs has come down a lot in recent years, and their accuracy has improved. A chronograph is a great investment for precision shooters and hunters.

In my experience, it is difficult to avoid handloading (reloading) if we want to achieve the best results in precision shooting. Handloading allows us to put together the components we like the best to suit a specific weapon and a specific shooting discipline. I don't have much to say about primers, powder, or bullets. There is of course a multitude of products on the market, and as many opinions about what is the best for a certain purpose. Choose what you think works well for your purposes. However, I want to mention a couple of important aspects of hand loading: *Cartridge Overall Length* (COL or COAL), *Cartridge Base to Ogive* (CBTO) and *ES: extreme spread.*

Cartridge length

A consistent cartridge length is vital for consistent precision in a rifle. Measuring the cartridge length is important to ensure consistency between cartridges. Measuring from the base of the bullet to the tip is not ideal, however, because the bullet tip on hunting or match bullets is usually not perfectly consistent. With Open Tip Match (OTM) bullets the differences in bullet length may be considerable. The best way to measure cartridge length is by measuring cartridge base to ogive (CBTO). For this purpose, we need specialty inserts that attach to a caliper, so that we can measure the distance from cartridge base to the ogive.

Both hunting and sport shooting rifles have slight differences in the dimensions of the chamber, and they react differently to varying cartridge length. However, what surprised me when I started testing different cartridge lengths is how much a rifle reacts to varying cartridge length. I don't mean mainly consistency in muzzle velocity but shot grouping. I have seen a couple of rifles go from a five-shot grouping of 40 mm to 15 mm (1.5 to .5 inches) at 100 meters (110 yd) just by changing the CBTO length by 1 mm (0.04 inches).

There are a few different schools of thought on testing for a cartridge length that your rifle likes, and I encourage you to seek out more information on that. I was taught how to do it by an old-timer who has forgotten more about shooting than I will probably ever know, and I'm passing that knowledge on to you. This method requires no special tools other than a reloading press, and is easy to do yourself. The first step is to measure the maximum length of the cartridge, before the bullet enters the lands of the barrel (maximum COL). This can be done in different ways, and there are special tool kits available. But one of the best ways is completely free and is done as follows:

- Disassemble the bolt: remove the firing pin and ejector so that the bolt can run freely and with minimal friction in the receiver.
- Assemble a cartridge *without powder or primer*. Using only the case and bullet, start by inserting the bullet very shallowly into the case with a reloading press.
- Insert the cartridge into the rifle and *carefully* try to insert the bolt into the gun and lock it. You won't be able to do this right away, because the bullet will hit the lands in the barrel. Keep seating the bullet a little bit deeper until you feel you can *almost close the bolt.*
- When you feel that you can almost close the bolt, reduce the total length of the cartridge by as little as you can in the loading press until you can close the bolt with minimal resistance.

Once this has been achieved, the maximum cartridge length for the specific weapon and bullet combination has been found. This provides a good starting point for testing the accuracy of different cartridge lengths. Note that the overall maximum cartridge length obtained by the method described above is usually unusable, because the cartridge is so long that it will not fit in a standard magazine. In rifles made for long range shooting, it is possible that they will fit in the magazine, but in hunting rifles the magazine is usually quite short. Some long-range shooters hold that you get better accuracy by loading long match bullets a bit into the lands, so that they have no free flight at all before they touch the lands. I haven't personally seen this improve accuracy in competition rifles, but this may be true for some rifle and bullet combinations. The disadvantage of loading bullets into the lands is that it may be difficult to extract the cartridge without the bullet separating from the brass, and the powder spilling into the gun's receiver. Such a scenario is obviously not desirable during competition or hunting, as it can be difficult to extract a bullet from the barrel.

Once we have determined the maximum cartridge length, we load five cartridges with a moderate amount of powder into the maximum cartridge length, or reduce the length to fit the magazine, depending on the weapon. We then reduce the cartridge length by one mm (0.04 inches) and load five cartridges with that measure as well. We continue reducing the CBTO length by 1 mm, loading 5 cartridges for each length, until the minimum length of the cartridge is reached. Once we have done this, we are ready to go to the range and test which cartridge length the rifle likes best. There are typically 20-30 cartridges in total to test fire. What always surprises me when I do this test is how much difference there is in precision between different cartridge lengths. There's always a cartridge length that a rifle prefers, and when we find it, it's like everything fits, and the grouping shrinks considerably. In my experience, hunting rifles and bullets do well with fairly short cartridge lengths, and competition rifles with longer bullets can shoot well with longer cartridge lengths. However, it is difficult to generalize, and we need to experiment to see how it works for a particular rifle.

Extreme spread

Extreme spread (ES) is a term used by competitive shooters and reloaders to refer to the maximum difference in muzzle velocity between a given number of rounds. Usually, five cartridges are used to measure ES, so ES in this case is the largest difference in muzzle velocity that can be observed within a group of five cartridges. As observed in the section on muzzle velocity and vertical dispersion above, differences in muzzle velocity can significantly affect bullet trajectory at longer distances. Measuring ES of cartridges requires access to a chronograph. However, when we compete in long-range shooting such an investment is small compared to its usefulness for long range accuracy.

I have mentioned these things about internal ballistics because they have a significant effect on the potential to achieve accuracy at longer ranges. I hope that you will benefit from this information if you are just starting to hand load, or intend to hand load your own ammunition.

COLLECTION OF FORMULAS

Ballistic coefficient

$$BC_{Projectile} = \frac{m/7000}{cal^2 \times i}$$

$BC_{Projectile}$ = the answer obtained from the equation in (US) pounds per square inch.

m = mass of the bullet in grain (gn). 1 grain = 0.0647989 grams

cal = caliber of bullet in inches

i = form factor or form coefficient

Form coefficient

$$i = \frac{C_p}{C_G}$$

i = Form coefficient or form factor (dimensionless value). It is the form coefficient that is later used to calculate the BC of a bullet.

C_p = drag coefficient of the projectile in question

C_G = drag coefficient of a standard projectile

Drag coefficient

$$C_{drag} = \frac{2F_d}{pu^2 A}$$

In which:

C_{drag} = Drag coefficient

F_d = Drag Force

p = density of the fluid (air)

u = velocity of the projectile in relation to the fluid

A = the reference area of the projectile (area where the fluid meets the projectile)

Drag

$$Drag = \frac{1}{2}\rho V^2 C_d A$$

In which:

ρ = density of the fluid

V = velocity of the fluid in relation to the projectile

C_d = drag coefficient

A = cross-sectional area of the projectile

Gyroscopic drift

$$Gyroscopic\ drift\ in\ cm =$$

$$3.175(Sg + 1.2)tof^{1.83}$$

In which:

3.175 = constant that gives the drift in cm; if you use 1.25 here you get the drift in inches

Sg = the gyroscopic stability factor according to the *Miller twist rule*. Below is a description of how to calculate your Sg for your current projectile/barrel combination. There is also an excellent calculator for this particular parameter on Berger Bullet's website that you can use to avoid having to calculate this equation yourself.

1.2 = another constant to be included

tof= *time of flight*, i.e. the flight time of the bullet at the distance for which you want to calculate the drift. This is most easily obtained by using a ballistic calculator.

1.83 = constant exponent

Gyroscopic stability factor

$$Sg = \frac{30m}{t^2 d^3 l(1 + l^2)}$$

In which:

Sg = gyroscopic stability factor

m = projectile weight in grains (gn)

t = barrel twist rate measured in number of calibers per revolution. "Caliber" here means the caliber of the weapon in which the projectile is shot in inches. For a 7.62 mm rifle, this value will be 0.30 inches.

d = diameter of the projectile measured in inches

l = length of the projectile measured in calibers

The horizontal component of the Coriolis effect

$$Coriolis\ drift\ in\ m =$$

$$0.000072 \times D \times \sin(Lat) \times tof$$

In which:

0.000072 = Earth's rotational speed in RAD/second

D = distance to target in meters

Sin(Lat) = sine of the latitude in degrees. The sine is a trigonometric function obtained by dividing the opposite side of the angle by the hypotenuse of the triangle.

tof = Time of flight in seconds

The Eötvös effect

$$F_c = 1 - \frac{2 \times 0.00007292 \times V_0}{9.806} \, \text{cosine}(Lat) \, \text{sine}(D)$$

In which:

F_c = correction factor by which data for projectile drop at a certain distance are multiplied to obtain the correct drop

0.00007292 = Earth's rotational speed (0.00007292 RAD per second)

V_0 = muzzle velocity of the projectile in meters per second

9.806 = standard measure of gravity

Lat = latitude from which to shoot

D = the direction of the shot in degrees (azimuth), counted clockwise from the North Pole

Horizontal distance to target

$$D_h = D_d \times cosine\ of\ angle$$

In which:
D_h = Horizontal distance

D_d = The diagonal (measured) distance

Lead for shooting moving targets

It doesn't matter if you use MRAD or MOA in the calculation, as long as you use one angular measurement consistently in the formula, it works.

$$Lead\ (MRAD) = target\ speed\ x\ tof$$

In which:

$target\ speed$ = number of MRAD/MOA the target moves per second

tof = flight time of the projectile to the target at the current distance.

Wind formulas

There are a number of formulas to calculate how much compensation is required for a given wind speed. Examples of such formulas are the British Wind Formula (for .308 Winchester), the Rule of 9s (for .308 Winchester), and the 6.5 mm formula. I tend to avoid using such formulas, as they are all generalizations that do not take into account a specific weapon and the parameters of the ammunition. Such formulas can, however, be useful if we should end up having to shoot with a weapon and ammunition that we are not familiar with, for whatever reason.

The 6.5 mm formula can be particularly useful, since the 6.5 Creedmoor and the 6.5x55 are very common calibers in the US and Europe respectively. The formula looks as follows:

6.5 mm formula

$$\frac{1}{10} MRAD = \frac{D}{100} \times \frac{W}{2}$$

In which:

$\frac{1}{10} MRAD$ = ballistic solution in 1/10 MRAD

D = Distance to target in meters

W = Wind speed in meters per second

For example, if the distance to the target is 600 meters ($\cong$660 yd) and the wind speed is 6 m/s, the formula is:

$$18 \, \frac{1}{10} MRAD \text{ (klick)} = \frac{600}{100} \times \frac{6}{2}$$

The answer is therefore that 18 clicks (1/10 MRAD) compensate for a full-value crosswind of 6 m/s at a distance of 600 meters. This formula is of course a generalization, as it does not take into account differences in ballistic coefficient or muzzle velocity of the projectile. But it is a decent formula if for some reason you do not have access to your ballistic tables when you are out shooting. It often delivers a result within a few clicks of what a ballistic calculator indicates, at least at medium distances.

CONVERSION OF UNITS OF MEASURE

As we all know, the world of hunting and shooting is dominated by American units. We Europeans have made a small gain with the increased use of MRAD (Milliradian) in general, and especially in long range shooting. Below is information for a shooter to be able to quickly convert between Imperial and Metric measurements.

Length measurements

1 inch = 2.54 cm

1 cm = 0.3937 inches

- To convert inches to cm: multiply X inches by 2.54
- To convert cm to inches: multiply X cm by 0.3937

1 yard = 0.9144 meter

1 meter = 1.0936 yards

- To convert yards to meters: multiply X yards by 0.9144
- To convert meters to yards: multiply X meters by 1.0936

1 mile = 1.609 km

1 km = 0.6213 mile

- To convert miles to km: multiply X miles by 1.609

- To convert km to miles: multiply X km by 0.6213

Projectile and wind speed

The velocity of projectiles is often given in fps (feet per second) in books and ballistic tables. It can be useful to be able to convert it to meters per second.

1 fps = 0.3048 m/s

1 m/s = 3.2808 fps

- To convert fps to m/s: multiply X fps by 0.3048
- To convert m/s to fps: multiply X m/s by 3.2808

Often when reading about wind in books or on the web, wind speed is given in miles per hour. It can be useful to be able to convert between mph and m/s.

1 mile per hour (mph) = 0.44 m/s

1 m/s = 2.23 mph

- To convert mph to m/s, multiply X mph by 0.44
- To convert m/s to mph: multiply X m/s by 2.23

Angular measurements

An angular measurement is a special type of tool used, for example, in distance assessment. Further discussion of angle measurement and how it works is given under the heading of Distance Assessment below.

1 MOA (*Minute of Arc / Minute of Angle*) = 0.290888 MRAD

1 MRAD (Milliradian) = 3.43775 MOA

- To convert MOA to MRAD: multiply *X* MOA by 0.290888
- To convert MRAD to MOA: multiply *X* MRAD by 3.43775

MOA adjustments are quite common on rifle scopes, such as ¼ MOA, or even 1/8 MOA on precision shooting scopes. It can be useful to be able to convert these measurements to cm at different distances.

1 MOA at 100 meters = 2.9082 cm

¼ MOA at 100 meters = 0.727 cm = 7.27 mm

1/8 MOA at 100 meters = 0.3635 cm = 3.635 mm

Since angular measurements increase linearly with distance, we only need to multiply the shooting distance in meters by 2.9082 to obtain the size of 1 MOA at that distance.

Table 63: Distance and MOA

Distance in meters	MOA
100 m	1 MOA = 2.90 cm
200 m	1 MOA = 5.81 cm
300 m	1 MOA = 8.72 cm
400 m	1 MOA = 11.63 cm
500 m	1 MOA = 14.54 cm
600 m	1 MOA = 17.44 cm
700 m	1 MOA = 20.35 cm
800 m	1 MOA = 23.26 cm
900 m	1 MOA = 26.17 cm
1000 m	1 MOA = 29.08 cm
1100 m	1 MOA = 31.99 cm
1200 m	1 MOA = 34.89 cm
1300 m	1 MOA = 37.80 cm
1400 m	1 MOA = 40.71 cm
1500 m	1 MOA = 43.62 cm

TOOLS AND AIDS

In this chapter I have collected some tools and techniques that I have accumulated over the years. I hope that they can be of use to you.

Distance assessment

The longer the distance, the more important it is to correctly estimate the distance to the target, as longer shots require more precise ballistic solutions to hit the target. In long-range rifle shooting competitions, we typically need some kind of system to measure or estimate the distance to the target, and laser rangefinders are typically not allowed. When competing with aperture (diopter) sights, the front sight is often used to measure the target and estimate the distance. When we use a reticle system in a rifle scope, the measurement works basically in the same way: we have a scale with lines in our scope with which we measure the target. We can then use a little mental arithmetic, or a table, to determine the distance to the target.

The reason it works to measure distance in the ways I have described above, is that there is predictability in how the eye perceives objects at different distances. For example, we perceive an object as twice as big when it is 100 meters away compared to 200 meters. Similarly, we perceive the object at 200 meters as half the size when it is at 400 meters. Since this perceived size of an object increases and decreases proportionally with distance, we can use various optical aids to measure the object, and then translate these measurements into real distances. To do this, we also need to know *at least one* measure of the target. We cannot estimate the distance of an unfamiliar object simply by measuring it with an angular measurement, because we have no frame of reference for how big such an object normally is. However, this is only in theory as most people have a rough estimate of how tall various objects are. But in precision shooting it is not enough to know *approximately* how high or wide the target is, we often need to know quite precisely in order to calculate the correct distances.

As I mentioned above, we can measure in different ways; we can do it with aperture sights, binoculars, rifle scopes or spotting scopes. For rifle scopes, there are two systems of angular measurements that dominate the market: these are the Milliradian (MRAD) and the Minute of angle/Minute of arc (or MOA). The milliradian is easier for Europeans because it is based on the metric system; one tenth of a milliradian is one cm at 100 meters. MOA is easier for Americans because it is close to, but not identical to, the inches and yards used in the United States.

Imagine a cone that has its tip at your eye, and the base of the cone has a diameter that increases with distance from you. At 100 meters the base of the cone is 10 centimeters, at 200 meters 20 centimeters, at 300 meters 30 centimeters, and so on. What you have just imagined is a milliradian (MRAD), which is a common angular measurement in shooting. An angular measurement is basically an imaginary elongated cone, where the diameter of the base increases linearly with distance. Angular measurements can be used in several ways in shooting. They are used to measure the distance to the target when at least one measure of the target is known in advance. They are also used to describe the accuracy of a weapon system; a rifle can be said to shoot "sub-MOA". This means that the rifle with three shots, or sometimes five shots, has a shot grouping no larger than 2.9 cm at one hundred meters (in the US it is usually 1 MOA at 100 yards).

The most important thing to keep in mind when measuring targets with optical aids and reticles is to have a stable platform. When measuring with aperture sights or a rifle scope, the weapon must be completely stable and stationary for the measurement to be correct. It is a great advantage if we can use different types of support for the weapon during the measurement, such as a bipod or a backpack in the front under the weapon, and a beanbag under the rear part of the stock to maximize stability. At longer distances it will still be difficult to measure correctly, even when we have good support. In competition we almost always have limited time to perform the measurement and are therefore stressed. Distance assessment is not something that should be rushed. It is a good idea to take the measurement twice, and to take a deep breath and exhale between measurements. *Breathing control is at least as important during distance assessment as during the actual shot.* I have seen experienced shooters shoot excellently without any particular breathing technique, and shooting at different stages of the breathing cycle. I have, however, never seen a shooter measure the distance to a target correctly without paying strict attention to breathing control. Even heartbeats typically disturb measuring of a distant target. If the target is bobbing up and down during the measurement, we will not get an accurate measurement to calculate the distance.

Using any of the methods I have described above are the most accurate ways to measure distances for shooting, after using laser rangefinders. However, in some situations like hunting it can be important to be able to judge distances in traditional ways, as shooters judged distances before laser rangefinders came onto the scene. Below are some traditional methods that we can use to estimate distance without aids.

Divide in half

We try to judge where the middle point is between us and the target, and then we estimate the distance to that point and multiply it by two. The reason why this method works is that it is more difficult to judge longer distances by eye than shorter ones. Above 400-500 meters or yards it is difficult to judge accurate distances by eye alone. Therefore, it is often easier to estimate the distance to the middle point between us and the target. However, this can be tricky and depends on the terrain and the altitude of the target, as discussed below in the section on sources of error in distance assessment.

Multiply a known length

The multiplication method involves the shooter taking a familiar phenomenon or object and trying to estimate how many of those objects would fit between themselves and the target. For many, this object is a football field, as most people have played football at some point. This method becomes more and more uncertain the longer the distances are, and above 400-500 meters it is no longer as good, but can be good enough depending on the purpose.

"Forking" the distance

Forking involves estimating a range of distances within which the target is believed to be located. We then take the middle of that range as the distance to the target. If we think the distance to a target is roughly between 400 and 600 meters, we adjust the sights to shoot at 500 meters. If we estimate that the target is somewhere between 800 and 1200 meters away, we adjust for 1000 meters. The method works because it forces the shooter to question their initial estimate of distance, and reflect on alternative assessments. If we quickly decide that we think the target is at a certain distance, it is easy to ignore common sources of error, which are discussed below.

Sources of error in distance assessment

Differing shooting circumstances will affect the eye's ability to accurately judge distance, and can cause errors. Once these errors are known, they can be compensated for when assessing distance. The guidelines below apply when we are trying to gauge a distance by eye only, and not using an angular measurement to do so.

The target is perceived to be closer than it actually is when:

- There is a gap in the ground between us and the target.
- We are located higher than the target.
- The ground between us and the target is flat, such as a field, water or a parking lot.

The target is perceived to be further away than it actually is when:

- The target is located higher than we are.
- The target is small in relation to its surroundings.
- We have a narrow field of view to see the target through, such as forest on both sides of the target.

Crosswind effect chart

I have constructed the tool below to quickly find the crosswind effect when shooting. You can copy or cut out the tool, laminate it and take it to the shooting range. A similar table using mph as measure of windspeed can easily be made according to the same design. Below the table is a description of how to use it.

			A	**N**	**G**	**L**	**E**				
			10°	20°	30°	40°	50°	60°	70°	80°	90°
W		1	0.2	0.4	0.5	0.7	0.8	0.9	1	1	1
		2	0.4	0.7	1	1.3	1.6	1.8	1.9	2	2
I		3	0.6	1.1	1.5	2	2.4	2.6	2.9	3	3
		4	0.7	1.4	2	2.6	3.1	3.5	3.8	4	4
N		5	0.9	1.7	2.5	3.2	3.9	4.3	4.7	4.9	5
		6	1.1	2.1	3	3.9	4.7	5.2	5.7	5.9	6
D		7	1.2	2.4	3.5	4.5	5.4	6.1	6.6	6.9	7
		8	1.4	2.8	4	5.2	6.2	6.9	7.6	7.9	8
S		9	1.6	3.1	4.5	5.8	7	7.8	8.5	8.9	9
		10	1.7	3.4	5	6.4	7.7	8.6	9.4	9.8	10
P		11	1.9	3.8	5.5	7.1	8.5	9.5	10.4	10.8	11
		12	2.1	4.1	6	7.7	9.3	10.4	11.3	11.8	12
E		13	2.3	4.5	6.5	8.4	10.1	11.2	12.3	12.8	13
		14	2.4	4.8	7	9	10.8	12.1	13.2	13.8	14
E		15	2.6	5.1	7.5	9.6	11.6	12.9	14.1	14.7	15
		16	2.8	5.5	8	10.3	12.4	13.8	15.1	15.7	16
D		17	2.9	5.8	8.5	10.9	13.1	14.7	16	16.7	17
		18	3.1	6.2	9	11.6	13.9	15.5	17	17.7	18
M/S		19	3.3	6.5	9.5	12.2	14.7	16.4	17.9	18.7	19
		20	3.4	6.8	10	12.8	15.4	17.2	18.8	19.6	20

CROSSWIND EFFECT ⟶

1. Assess the wind speed with an anemometer or by other means.

2. Assess the angle of the wind to the line of sight between you and the target. This can be done approximately or more accurately by using a compass, wind vane or just by throwing some grass up in the air and seeing which way the wind is blowing. What I've done is to laminate a picture of a protractor behind the table itself so that they are one unit. I can read the approximate angle of the protractor, and

then turn it over and see directly in the table what the crosswind effect is.

3. Look in the left column of the table for your measured or assessed wind speed, and follow that row to the right until you meet the column for your estimated wind angle relative to the bullet trajectory. The correct crosswind effect is in the box where the row and column meet. Now you can adjust for the correct crosswind effect, according to the caliber that you are shooting.

You can of course develop a similar table and directly enter your correct adjustments in milliradians (MRAD) or minutes of angle (MOA) into it to make the process even faster. I haven't done this, because I tend to change loads from time to time, and don't want to have to rewrite tables as it is quite time consuming. I personally like to use colors in my tables because colors can help to give a quicker idea of the size of the drift, but I also realize that colors can cause problems for people who suffer from color blindness. For them, a more neutral color scale in tables may be better. Note that the last three columns in the crosswind effect chart are all in red. This is because the difference in crosswind effect between 70 and 90 degrees is so minute that all winds over 70 degrees to the trajectory are very close to full wind value. The red color is simply to remind myself of that fact, and to treat all winds over 70 degrees to the trajectory basically as a full-value wind.

Determining wind speed

Below is a table that can help determine wind speed based on observations at the shooting location. Note that plants, shrubs and trees tend to react differently to differing wind speeds depending on where they grow. For example, trees and shrubs in windswept mountainous environments tend to grow lower and stiffer and are more resistant to swaying in the wind. Similar species on a lower altitude often grow taller and sway more in the same wind speed. One conclusion from this is that we need to know the environment we are assessing the wind in. It is advisable to reconnoiter the environment in advance with a wind meter to see how different species of trees and shrubs behave at different wind speeds. Normally, shooting in wind speeds above 10 m/s (22 mph) is very difficult, and above 15 m/s (33 mph) something of a lottery, especially at very long distances. However, it is of course fun to challenge ourselves to shoot in powerful winds.

Table 64: wind speed indicators

Description	mph	m/s	Indicators
Calm	< 1 mph	< 0.5 m/s	No sign of wind. Mirage rises straight up and leaves do not move.
Light air	1-3 mph	0.5–1.5 m/s	We feel the wind on our face when we stand up or walk.
Light Breeze	4–7 mph	1.6–3.3 m/s	Leaves, foliage, and thin twigs begin to move.
Gentle breeze	8–12 mph	3.4–5.5 m/s	The wind stretches a pennant, setting leaves and thin twigs in continuous motion.
Moderate breeze	13–18 mph	5.6–7.9 m/s	Twigs and thin branches move. Dust and loose snow swirl up.
Fresh breeze	19–24 mph	8–10.7 m/s	Smaller trees begin to sway.
Strong breeze	25–31 mph	10.8–13.8 m/s	Large tree branches are set in motion. Telephone wires whine.
Moderate gale	32–38 mph	13.9–17.1 m/s	Whole trees begin to sway. We cannot walk unhindered against the wind.
Gale, Fresh gale	39–46 mph	17.2–20.7 m/s	Branches are breaking off the trees and it is becoming difficult to walk in the open.

BIBLIOGRAPHY

McCoy, Robert L. - Modern external ballistics: the launch and flight dynamics of symmetric projectiles (1999)

McDonald, William T. and Almgren, Ted C. - The Ballistic Coefficient (2008)

Litz, Bryan - Applied Ballistics for Long Range Shooting 3rd Edition: Understanding the Elements and Application of External Ballistics for Successful Long-Range Target Shooting and Hunting (2015)

Cleckner, Ryan - Long Range Shooting Handbook: Complete Beginner's Guide to Long Range Shooting (2016)

Geurtjens, Jeremy - Practical Long Range Shooting (2019)

Persson, Anders - How Do We Understand the Coriolis Force? European Centre for Medium-Range Weather Forecasts, Reading, Berkshire, United Kingdom (1998)

Persson, Anders O. - The Coriolis Effect: Four centuries of conflict between common sense and mathematics, Part I: A history to 1885, History of Meteorology 2 (2005)

Herrera, Eduardo and Morett, Sigrid - On the direction of Coriolis force and the angular momentum conservation, Revista Brasileira de Ensino de F´ısica, vol. 38, n° 3, e3304 (2016)